The Story So Far

An Anthology of Poetry and Life

by

Graham Woodall

First Edition: 2010 (November)
Revised 2010 (December)

ISBN: 978–0–9556771-3-7

www.lulu.com

FOREWORD

Between the years 1967 and 2007 I was engaged in the writing of a book which was published in December2007 with the title of **Across my World.**

'What sort of a book takes forty years to write?', you may well ask.

'Not much of a book.', I may well reply.

Needless to say, it was not exactly a full time job for those forty years. However, in some ways it was just that. I spent about an hour in 1967 working on it then a couple of hours in 1979 and couple more in both 1982 and 1988. The next flurry of writing was in the mid- 1990s, leaving the bulk to be done in the new millennium. But the writing of a book is the easy bit, the rest of the time was in effect doing the research although I didn't realise that was what I was doing until early 2007. In this case, the research constituted very little more than living a very full and enjoyable but otherwise ordinary life, because the subject of the book was very largely my experiences of that life, expressed in the form of a series of poems. Since the first poem in 1967 I had always been inclined to note events and feelings in verse form, usually kept to myself like diary entries, and not in all cases recorded on paper.

I should say at this point that I have been blessed with an extraordinary memory which started sketchily with the 1954 F.A. Cup Final and then continued with more detail through the birth of my sister a year or so later and so on until about Christmas 1958 since when I have remembered just about everything that I found of interest or amusement at the time. Certain things that were neither interesting nor amusing have also been inadvertently committed to memory and some stuff has even been remembered out of strict necessity. My sister claimed, some years ago, that her memory was full and that she had to forget something already there before she was able to store anything knew. I didn't understand why she thought that at the time as I had always been led to believe that the human brain has an unlimited storage capacity. Over the past four or five years I have come to agree with her conclusion as I find that it takes me a lot of effort to learn things these days and although I can instantly recall tiny events from 1961, I struggle to recall what I had for lunch yesterday

Anyway, a dozen or more such poems, those composed years ago, were cast aside or forgotten as the passage of time dulled the feelings of passion, disappointment or whatever had inspired the writing in the first place.

As a result of this, as you may have noticed from the dates given above, next to nothing remains of the 1970s despite the fact that it and the decade which followed were probably the most eventful of my entire life in terms of not only the number of things that happened to me but also in terms of the significance of those events.

In or about 2005, I established contact with a second cousin on my father's side of the family, Tina Negus, for the first time although I had known her parents very well when I was a child and had visited them several times in my teens and early twenties. Tina, it transpired, is a prolific poet and this discovery inspired me to dig out as many of my old poems as I could find (from boxes in the loft as well as from the depths of my memory) and also to enter another creative phase by writing some new ones.

I had always had a fascination with the First World War because it was a major event in history that stood alongside the Battle of Hastings, the end of Charles the First, the abolition of the monasteries and so on but it was also within the personal memory of many people who were still alive and whom I knew well.

On the other hand, the Second World War had not by then passed into history as such, having been so recent as to almost qualify as 'current affairs'. The bomb sites were still there to be seen, air raid shelters were still being used as coal sheds and the everyday conversations of many people around me still referred to the war as a matter of course. Many still wore clothing that had covered them during the long nights in the same air raid shelters.

As it was with many other people, the Great War was of particular interest to me because of the poetry that it inspired. The combination of this and my newly re-kindled interest in poetry inevitably led to me write **Pity**. However, this was soon followed by *Isandlwana* which was actually a re-working of what I could remember of something I had written many years earlier after seeing the film **Zulu**. I therefore spent much of 2006 writing poems or recalling and revising ones written years before and then much of 2007 assembling them into book form by adding introductory notes to each.

This then was the culmination of forty years research and writing and I called it **Across my World** after the first line of one of the poems, as is explained in the text. The publication was actually delayed a while by the illness and subsequent death of my father, the incomparable Dennis Woodall, and this filled me with resolve to bring out another book within the year in the hope that the writing of it would act as a therapy for me to help the grieving process and as a distraction from the realisation that I had become an orphan, my mother having died seventeen years earlier.

I almost succeeded but then made the mistake of deciding to add photographs to illustrate the text. This decision gave me all sorts of technical problems which combined with life events to result in a draft publication in mid 2009 followed by more revisions and additions before inflicting it on the public in 2010. I called this one *Out of the Shadow* using the same line of poetry that contained 'across my world', with the shadow in question this time being not any war but the sadness of losing my dear old Dad.

As you will read later, I have a certain fondness for the music of Ralph McTell. Ralph published his autobiography in two volumes called, respectively, *Angel Laughter* and *Summer Lightning.* Much later he combined both of these into a new book which he called *As far as I can tell.* It is undeniable that my own two volumes are partial autobiographies and as there were several spelling errors in the first one and several passages of text in the second one with which some people who I would not wish to upset could easily take offence, I decided to follow Ralph's example and revise both of them into what could be described as an omnibus edition. The controversial passages have been left out. The spelling errors have been corrected (or, more likely, replaced with new ones) and in a few cases I have added some comment of the structure of the poems themselves to the explanations as to how each came to have been written. In places I have updated or simply added to the narrative that was written previously. Lastly. I have added several poems that have either been written since *Out of the Shadow* or were left out of that and *Across my World* for one reason or another. That takes the total number of poems into three figures.

The title, *The Story So Far* bravely, and perhaps foolishly, assumes that there will be more to follow later. This is not an echo of Wordsworth's *Prelude* as one thing I am sure of is that my life has been the real thing, not a curtain raiser for something else and certainly not just a rehearsal. *Prelude* took Wordsworth several decades to write and it was continuously being revised throughout that time. It was never published in Wordsworth's lifetime whereas I sincerely hope that this work will be. My life has not so far been a prelude to anything other than the next chapter of it.

This is *The Story so Far.* Please read and enjoy.

CONTENTS:

The Sisi Set:

'2020 Vision' is, perhaps, a contrived title based upon a well known expression indicative of good eyesight. However, it suits the piece in two ways and may convey some idea of how I expect the World to look by the end of the second decade of the 21st Century.

Orwell's *'1984'* was regarded by many as his vision of the World in that year. In truth it was his interpretation of what the world looked like at the time of writing. This was 1948, but to avoid political controversy so soon after the Second World War had fragmented into a series of more local conflicts, he simply changed the order of the last two digits and, by doing so, came to sound like a prophet

Perhaps then, *'2020 Vision'* is how I see the World already. The Fourth World is a place inhabited by has-been nations; former leaders such as England having been replaced in prime position from the end of the 19th century by the New World led by the USA. Third World nations are taking their turn on the ascendancy and ancient civilisations such as China and India, without thus far resorting to conventional war, are poised to take the benefits and comforts that had yet to be discovered or invented when they were leaders of a civilised world before the rise of the European nations. For a decade before the date that this poem was written, England had been led by those who saw themselves as World Statesmen eager to stake their place in history on an international stage at the expense of those at home. Far better for them to be seen helping America to blast Iraq into oblivion than at home looking after the interests of the innocent souls who elected them into office and who now have to pay for the bombs. Along with education and other essentials, the National Health Service of which we in Britain were once so proud has, despite the huge sums of hard earned public money being thrown at it, been allowed to wither to the point where it seems that only private health care can be relied upon other than in emergencies. This has to be paid for by the individual who has also contributed to the NHS kitty out of already taxed earnings.

The poem itself is of course a sonnet in what I call the Sicilian style, with its regular metre and end rhymes. Apart from a couple of alliterations to look out for in lines nine and eleven, no further analysis is necessary.

2020 Vision

So now the English enter the Fourth World:
the New one rules for now but, soon, the Third.
Around the globe the Jack was once unfurled
by subjects of the Crown, as free as birds.
Now ancient countries rise again to match
emerging nations on the great ascent
that leads to domination of the patch
once ruled by Europeans, heaven sent.
The sun has set on empires that were proud
to exploit others in their quest for wealth.
Its light now shines for those who shout out loud
but take the power less by force than stealth.
Yet still our leaders seek to please the crowd,
with foreign aid whilst we pay twice for health.

One evening in the early part of 2006 I sat down with a glass of wine, Wolf Blass Yellow Label Cabernet Sauvignon if you must know, to watch the 10 'o' clock news on BBC. The lead item, untypically as I care little about many of the items that news editors seem to think matter, was of interest to me as it reported the death of John Profumo. Mr. Profumo was a politician of the highest order who fell from grace in 1963 for doing nothing worse than lying to the House of Commons. The same rule applied to everyone would empty about 500 seats these days but his indiscretion had national security implications at the height of the Cold War so he had to go. The matter involved the death of a socialite osteopath, the fall of the Conservative Government to enable the disastrous Wilson era to begin and made household names of a couple of young ladies of dubious morals. The ubiquitous Lord Denning also played a part. Books were written and films made. Throughout the scandal, Profumo's wife, herself a former film star, remained loyal to him and although his political career was over for ever he continued, with her support, in various charitable works right up to his death. To some extent, the Establishment appeared to forgive him eventually. Others such as Paddy Ashdown and John Major at home, and Bill Clinton on the international stage have shown that the general public sometimes prefers a politician with a touch of sparkle to a squeaky-clean grey figure.

The time was also of enormous personal significance to me. I was entering the grown-up world of secondary school education and, like millions of my contemporaries, becoming increasingly fond of a quartet of young musicians from Liverpool who themselves were to change the World forever over the following few years. I have a photograph taken by my grandfather, Harold Woodall, whilst we were on holiday in Margate, showing me outside a hotel in which some of the Great Train Robbers were in hiding. They were arrested a few days later and a similar photograph, but without me on it, appeared in the national press. The year ended with the assassination of President Kennedy.

The sonnet 'Dear John' sums up 1963 as I recall it. It is written in the form of a letter from me to Mr Profumo and is in the Shakespearean style of rhyming pattern which differs slightly from the Sicilian style of the previous poem. This one also draws slightly on enjambment or run on at line ends which, when read out loud, breaks up the 'dee dah dee dah' rhythm to some extent.

Dear John,

Commencing at Cliveden, home of Astor,
a lovely young girl was taken upon
the ride that led to major disaster
for Britain, Stephen and maybe you, John.
A Russian and you were rivals in fun
but the Bay of Pigs was still in the news.
Lies you told, later copied by Clinton
and Valerie showed that Hobson can choose.
Mandy Rice Davies and Denning the Law
joined with the cast on this memorable stage.
Buster and Biggs and the Fabulous Four
with Kennedy's death then took the front page.
Now you have gone in the physical sense
you will be remembered, fifty years hence.

Graham.

4

It was in the late Summer of 2001 that I decided to register with the 'dot com' phenomenon that was 'Friends Reunited'. My niece, Clare Hanson, had mentioned it to me few weeks earlier but I had never found the spare time to check it out. Then my life-long friend, Ian Fellows, gave me a demonstration of it on his lap-top computer after lunch one Sunday and I was hooked. I joined in the very next day. For my part this led to the resumption of many friendships that had started at West Bromwich Grammar School almost 40 years earlier and to the forging of many new friendships with non-contemporaries from the same school.

These friendships were corollaries of a huge reunion that a few of us, including Ian, organised in July 2002 to mark the Centenary of the founding of that school. In the cases of some of those attending, romantic relationships rather than simple friendships were either renewed or brought to belated fruition. I understand that such developments were repeated in connection with schools from up and down the country and indeed world-wide. Sometimes, marriages were ruined and families broken up for the want of satisfying a twenty year or much longer lasting crush on a former class-mate. Not having trodden fresh romantic ground myself for many a long year, I wondered how sweethearts from the dim and distant past went about repeating or re-enacting the courtship rituals that we all did as second nature in our youth.

The thought of Spring love in the Autumn of life intrigued me and led to the writing of **'Equinox'**. The working title was actually 'Which Equinox?' to reflect my initial assumption that these dear old souls were, in reality, deluded as to which end of their metaphoric lifespan of a year they were nearer to. As the poem evolved, however, a clearer picture emerged for me and proved the old adage correct; you are only as old as you feel. But remember! Do I always write the truth?

Equinox

Can love lie sleeping, unfulfilled
for forty years or more
and then awake like Spring soil, tilled,
more fruitful than before?

Can hearts combine to beat as one
when weakened by life's tasks?
The passion of young life not gone,
the wrinkles only masks.

Can limbs entwine, that never did,
those urges now to meet
or, as before, must thoughts be hid
within those dreams, so sweet?

Can life be short, as so it seems
as shadows lengthen now,
or is there more beyond those beams
when from this stage we bow?

The answers rest with you my friend
and you and you and you.
For all us lovers know our end
and chances are but few.

I was fortunate enough, in those bomb-site scarred, half-rationed days of austerity that followed World War Two, to be born in the town of West Bromwich in the heart of England. As a direct result of this, as inevitably that night will follow day, I became a follower of West Bromwich Albion Football Club. It was a very successful club in those days, and had already been such for about 80 years, playing at the same home ground since 1900. The glory days continued intermittently until about 1985 when serious decline set in and this decline has still to be fully reversed. In one of the best periods in history for the Club, a young player from Chester-le-Street, in the North East of England, Bryan Robson, started his career with the Club. He married a local girl who happened to be of my acquaintance, and adopted both town and club as second homes, possibly third homes if you include Manchester, where he was taken when Ron Atkinson became manager of one of the clubs there. Bryan achieved massive success as a player and became an England Captain of great renown.

In 2004 Bryan became Manager of West Bromwich Albion F.C who were struggling to hold on to the place in the top division of English football that they had gained the season before. Whilst some die-hards in the crowd had never forgiven Bryan for leaving the Club years earlier, he was generally regarded as the right man for the job and a wave of optimism for the future of the Club was sustained when relegation was avoided that season. Bottom of the division at the halfway stage, they performed what came to be called *'The Great Escape'*. However, this was only temporary and the following season saw re-entry into the lower division. Soon after the start of the 2006/07 season he was asked to leave. This necessitated a revision to *'The Hawthorns'*, which was originally written to mark his appointment, with the following prophetic last four lines...

'Now Bryan's back, a hero with Great Ron,
whose football talents we can see no more.
For on the field he stood above the rest
but on the line he's yet to stand the test.'

Again, the form is Shakespearean with enjambment.

The Hawthorns

The hallowed turf, where mighty men have trod,
is called The Hawthorns or, by some, The Shrine.
And battles have been staged upon this sod
on many days since eighteen ninety nine.
Pennington, Bassett, Bomber and The King
were all great heroes in their time but, since
those glory years, with Willy on the wing,
the faithful few would settle for a prince.
Pretenders to the throne have been and gone
but none has matched the heady heights of yore.
When Bryan came, we thought he was the one
but now his tactics we shall see no more.
For on the field he stood above the rest
but on the line he didn't stand the test

As you may read later, I once spent a holiday in the Austrian region of Salzkammergut, in awe of the lakes and mountains. Soon after returning to England I recalled that it had been many years since I had visited our own Lake District and so Denise and I booked into a hotel in Grasmere for a short stay. I quickly recalled why we had been to the trouble and expense of the journey to Austria as, by comparison to Wolfgangsee and its neighbours, Windermere is now an over-commercialised boating pond with even its swans trained to tamely take tourists' feed, and the hills around it comprise little more than rising shores. Grasmere remains largely unspoilt and whilst both its waters and hills are beautiful and evocative of tranquil stability, the inspiration for poetry that I was expecting to overwhelm me with ideas never quite materialised.

This expectation was of course based upon the reputations of William Wordsworth, Samuel T Coleridge and the like; poets from the romantic period forever associated with that region. In truth, I knew little of their work beyond 'I wandered lonely as a cloud', a poem that was more or less compulsory learning for school children of my era. I assumed that in the late 18th and early 19th century not only was the area more stunningly beautiful than it is now in absolute terms but also that the likes of Wordsworth would have lacked the experience of having seen bigger and better versions in Italy, Austria and elsewhere. I can travel, door to door, from my home in Staffordshire to a hotel in Salzburg in a single morning but Wordsworth had no such advantages. He must, I thought, have been so taken by these English lakes and hills that they provided him with sufficient inspiration and interest to fuel a very long lifetime of writing poetry. How wrong I was!!

Inspiration did come after a day or two but in a sadly negative way: I found myself writing a poem that set out to bring Wordsworth down from the pedestal upon which he had been set a century or more before my birth. It was abandoned after the first few lines that went something like this...........

Wordsworth was a one-trick pony
'Daffodils' and not much more.
Even those words were on loan, he
took them from his sister, Dor.
His 'Prelude' was a tiresome story,
far too long and just a bore.

I visited Dove Cottage where he lived for many years and which is now part of a museum complex with a bookshop. I always find it physically impossible to enter any bookshop and leave empty-handed. I therefore became equipped with a couple of anthologies of Wordsworth's work, together with a biography. I found that he had written over 400 sonnets, a favourite poetic form of mine too, and volume after volume of other work. I cannot say that I was converted to being a Wordsworth devotee, as I would not describe more than about one fifth of the total as being to my taste. However, it did become clear to me that he was not the parochial bumpkin that I had taken him to be, by a country mile! He did live a long life, dying soon after his 80th birthday, and he did spend a great deal of it in the English Lake District. However, what I had not previously realised was that, in his younger days, he and a friend had WALKED about 3000 miles in 12 weeks to see, amongst other sights, the Alps, the Saint Gothard Pass and the Italian lakes. With the same friend he also spent a great deal of time in the Snowdon area of Wales, taking in more splendid views, and he was therefore at least as well informed as a post World War II baby-boomer like me, and all without my advantages of jet powered aeroplanes and high speed trains. It wasn't all sight-seeing either. For a start, the said friend, a Robert Jones, had no less than three single and available sisters at home whilst Wordsworth was staying in Wales!

During his 'Grand Tour' he had developed a relationship with a French girl, Annette Vallon, which had resulted in the birth of his first child, Caroline, in late 1792. To add to the romance of it all, England and France went to war in February 1793 thus preventing him from returning to France for many years or, perhaps, giving him the perfect excuse not to! One can only speculate as to the goings-on at Dove Cottage, which appears to have been transformed at times into an opium den by Coleridge.

Against this background and his years at Cambridge University, he could not be regarded by any means as being unworldly and I considered that it behove me to cease work immediately on the untitled poem I had begun and to write something much more respectful. I decided to convert him to a First World War poet travelling again, this time as a ghost, through Europe in 1918 or thereabouts.

The result was *"The Spirit of Wordsworth'* and any similarity it may have to his *'Daffodils'* in terms of its form is purely intentional!

10

The Spirit of Wordsworth

I floated wanly in my shroud,
without the Opium-eater's pills,
and saw the poppies growing proud
like ghosts of dancing daffodils.
A million men brought to their knees
and then to die with rats and fleas.

Those blood-red blooms were not in line
but, scattered, sprang forth from the clay.
Their simple splendour was a sign
that should our fear of death allay.
A sign that life came not by chance,
that loveless landscape to enhance.

As I beheld this bright array,
the blackened branches of a tree
returned me to the fearsome fray
fought, some had said, to make them free.
Did all that crimson come to nought
just like before, when France we fought?

A hundred years had passed since I
bore witness to an earlier feud.
Another score and, from the sky,
the rain of death shall there be viewed.
Is it eternal that Man kills
to save his own, or take his thrills?

I have often found that the inspiration or idea for a poem comes from another, sometimes also written by me as will be seen, but usually from one or more written by others. *'Historic Journey'* claims its parentage from both of these sources.

Having written **'The Spirit of Wordsworth'**, a poem that casts William Wordsworth as a Great War poet, I decided to create a connection between Wordsworth and the man who for me is the greatest of Great War poets, Wilfred Owen.

It is well known that Owen, possibly shell-shocked, possibly concussed from a fall or possibly for some other reason, was sent to Craiglockhart Hydropathic Establishment in Edinburgh for treatment by Dr. Rivers. Here, he became editor of the house journal and, through it, his own first publisher. He also met Siegfried Sassoon there and their friendship was very influential on Owen's work and life, short that it was to be afterwards. Sassoon was at best bisexual and many friends and acquaintances to whom he introduced Owen had even clearer preferences for same-sex relationships. Owen didn't live long enough for conclusions to be reached either way and the sexual orientation of Dr. Rivers is not entirely clear.

Owen travelled North by train to Edinburgh's Waverley Station and, not surprisingly, slept through much of the long journey, passing close to the region of his childhood on the way. It is not a giant leap of the imagination to say that in his dreams he may have stopped off in the Lake District, a few miles south of his eventual destination, to meet some predecessor poets and to share with them his habitual cigarettes, although possibly enhanced in flavour and effect by Coleridge.

In addition to having the sonnet form, Sicilian this time, favoured by both Wordsworth and Owen, **'Historic Journey'** makes deliberately exaggerated use of what Poet Laureate John Masefield once called Owen's 'continuous alliterative assonance'. End of line rhymes as such have thereby been deliberately avoided. I can confidently leave the many other allusions in this poem for the reader to find.

Historic Journey

The time when Wilfred went by Windermere,
a wet and windswept weekend whilst unwell,
Craiglockhart was the place to clear the mire
that wound his wits into a woolly whirl.
His train, Waverley-bound, sent him to sleep
but in his dreams he saw the waters, calm,
and vales of browning leaves beneath the slope
of soaring hillsides he would never climb.

In reverie he met the Grasmere Set,
took poppies with his Gold Flake, as they did
and, with Dove Cottage as his dugout, sat
to wonder who still lived and who was dead.
By Dunbar's shores he woke and smoothed his suit
and went to Rivers, straight in thought and deed.

I have already mentioned the Centenary Reunion of my old school.

When the school was founded, in 1902, a language teacher by the name of John Carroll joined the Staff and stayed for 35 years. In 1906 his French wife presented him with a daughter who later attended the same school before taking a degree at Birmingham University and subsequently becoming a major film star with over forty leading parts to her credit in films ranging from *'The Guns of Loos'* to Hitchcock's *'The Thirty Nine Steps'*. She was Madeline Carroll and she was at one time described as being the most beautiful woman in the World. Her nationality remains the subject of some debate, varying between that of her father, that of her mother, that of her birth, that of her various husbands and that of her various residences. Probably for that reason, she was never officially honoured by Britain, as would certainly be expected by a star of half her magnitude today, for no reason other than for being famous. This was despite the fact that she effectively foreshortened her glittering career in favour of charitable work during World War II.

Old Throstles, as former pupils of the said school are known, have tried in some way to give her the recognition we think she deserves and to supplement similar aspirations by a local historian, Terry Price, an admirer who has been successful in placing a monument and various commemorative plaques in her honour in the town of her birth. Her graduation from Birmingham University in 1926 was commemorated on the Roll of Honour of the old school and remains to this day.

She was 23 years older than my mother and although her life overlapped mine by about 35 years, we never met but I have had the honour and pleasure to have met her cousin, Ciaran O'Carroll who takes an interest in both the town and the school where his Uncle Jack lived and worked, and in preserving the memory of his cousin.

My own contribution to her centenary year in 2006 was a poem which requires little further explanation other that to mention that although my head has been almost completely hair-free for some years, it was once described by Thomas Turner, another Old Throstle and Chairman of the School Governors when I was a pupil, as 'a field of corn'.

Once more we have a simple Sicilian sonnet.

Sonnet to an Old Throstle

Oh Madeleine, why were you there so soon?
At twice my mother's age when I was born
there never was a chance that you might swoon
to see my golden hair – a field of corn!
The guns of Loos fired in my granddad's time,
your film of them came when his son was four.
The Tower opened with you in your prime,
they queued on ev'ry step up to the door.
Old Throstles saw you forming as a bud
that blossomed fully when you crossed the foam.
By then you'd left this land for Hollywood
but further conflict started close to home
so greater fortunes you trod in the mud
as battlefields of Europe you would roam.

'Janus' is another example of one poem inspiring another.

In choosing the title for *'Equinox'*, it occurred to me that, as the word itself signifies the two occasions each year when the day and the night are of equal length, why then does the 'nox' dominate? I have no idea what the true answer to that question might be although I have little doubt that there is such an answer. It did give me the idea to write about all sorts of situations in which the same basic fact could be viewed in two directly opposite ways, according to the mood or personality of the party involved. The working title for the poem was *'Equidies'* with the intention of balancing up the general and common over-use of the word 'equinox'.

However, thoughts of Janus, the two faced creature of mythology, rose to the surface during the writing stage and so that is what it came to be called. It starts with the familiar analogy of the glass which appears half empty to one person and half-full to another. It then proceeds to raise equivalent questions about a whole raft of situations from daily life, some of which probably never occur outside my own head.

I encourage the feeding of Robins, Blue Tits, Finches, Sparrows and the like in my own garden, even the widely despised Magpie, but yet I have to resist the temptation to take an air rifle to Pigeons. Why should that be? Is a male-dominated nursery rhyme still sexist when the boy comes a cropper before the girl?

I shall leave the other lines unexplained, the poem is simple enough without me spelling out even the less-obvious meanings; I must leave something to the imagination of the reader

Janus

Is the glass half empty or half full?
Is to work a curse or a treat?
Does Summer rain refresh or annoy?
Does a draw equate to defeat?

Is fifty five into middle age?
Is three score years and ten enough?
Does it feel warm for the time of year?
Does living a soft life feel tough?

Is the baking Sun the farmer's friend?
Is a rainy July preferred?
Does a 'B' grade make you smile or frown?
Does a pigeon rank as a bird?

Is a long, dark night cosy and snug?
Is a Winter's day far too short?
Does cooking at home become a chore?
Does home-made taste better than bought?

Is sowing or reaping better loved?
Is a hard place better than rocks?
Does Jack beat Jill, falling downhill?
Does Equidies beat Equinox?

'Summer of Love' has a claim to being the first of my serious poems. It was written in 1967 and, for reasons long since forgotten if ever known, it was originally entitled **'Napoleon Complex'**. By the time I revised the work circa 1982, 'the summer of love' was the definitive description of 1967 and also summed up the prevailing mood at the time I wrote the words. Hence the title. It can also lay claim to being the first of a very small number of my poems that was actually commissioned. My close friend and cultural guru, Alan Cartwright, was compiling an anthology to which he was intending to give the rather presumptuous title of 'The Rubber Hat of Omar Cartwright'', presumably also intending to give appropriate acknowledgement to Mr. Kayam, and was looking for contributions. I don't think that book was ever completed but if it was then I am absolutely certain that it would not have contained a single rubai, unlike this one that has five!

In those days I used to spend many hours in Dartmouth Park, West Bromwich, with various friends including Alan. On one such occasion I came upon an old man, probably a tramp but not begging, and I developed an irresistible urge to help him. In my pocket I had a pound note and a two shilling piece. Secure in the knowledge that I would be able to purchase the latest Beatles record, a packet of cigarettes, a couple of pints of beer and still have change from the pound note, I gave the man the coin. The intention was good but my clumsy execution of the gift is not something of which I should be particularly proud. I did no more than toss the money to him with the condescending shout of "Here, Mate, get yourself some dinner". He could have bought a fish and chips meal, as was my wish, but alternatively he could have bought a pint of beer or ten cigarettes and it did occur to me that both of the last two options would be more likely than the first. He was therefore very much like me whilst remaining very much like the bee I was watching earlier – eagerly taking what he needed from what he found in the park. My use of the word 'trudging' was not consciously taken from Owen's **'Dulce et Decorum est'**, it was a word that was frequently used by my mother and by her mother. The phrase 'pound in my pocket' pre-dated Wilson's devaluation speech by several months.

I had no way of knowing it at the time but the image of that man remains with me still and came to the fore many years later when he became the subject of a second poem, **'The Old Soldier'**.

Summer of Love

Here I sit on a hot, sultry day
watching a bee buzzing around
on thin, delicate wings.
I see a man, a tired old man
trudging in thin, delicate boots
and carrying a worn out raincoat
out of habit, not need, this fine day.
The pound in my pocket will be spent
on cigarettes and beer and music.
"Baby you're a rich man" sings John
and he's right – he always is.
The florin I fling with kind contempt
will buy food for the man today.
Or will it? I must wonder.
Are we so different, the man, the bee and I?

I can't remember a time when I was not a fast runner. I am sure there must have been such a time because, when I was very young, I had to go to bed each night with metal splints strapped to my legs to straighten them. They said I was 'knock kneed' but all that I can recall of that time was the name of the consultant, Mr Kirkham, whom I visited at the local hospital every now and then and who, I presume, eventually decreed that it would be alright for me to sleep like normal people do. I estimate that I would have been five years old when the treatment ended.

The next related situation that remains in my memory can be placed in the summer in which I reached the age of seven and this was the winning of a model aeroplane by coming first in a race against the other boys in my school year. I continued to win such races annually but at all other times I ran just for the fun of running, without competition and without any good reason to do it other than that I found walking boring. As a matter of fact I still do find walking boring but it has been at least twenty years since I last dared to break into as much as a trot in public, except once to catch a train. During the last couple of years at Grammar School I recorded some very good times for the 100 and 220 yards races and, later, the 100 and 200 metres races. I could just about complete 400 metres in less than one minute with heavy breathing but beyond that my lungs and legs gave out more or less simultaneously. I did enrol at Birchfield Harriers, as it was close to where I had started working for a living, when I left school with the intention of taking athletics seriously the following summer. Apparently my times were comparable with several others who went on to do quite well, including my very close contemporary, Alan Wells, who won Olympic Gold for the 100 metres in Moscow although it must be said first that he was a long jump specialist rather than a pure sprinter as a teenager and, second, that the Americans had boycotted the Olympics that year so his competition was diminished to some extent.

We shall never know what might have been but as I stopped growing at about that time, having started young, my own belief is that I would soon have been overtaken by my contemporaries as their legs became longer than mine. Much the same applies to the high jump as although I could jump my own height, that was only a winning formula for so long as I was taller than the others. Mind you, the real end to my high jumping career came with the 1968 Olympics when Dick Fosbury startled the World with his new style of jumping which became known as the Fosbury Flop and which is pretty much the style that has been used ever since. My only attempt at using that style very nearly broke my neck so that was the end of that.

20

The end of my athletics career, well more or less then end as I did run in my firm's sports day once and then a few times in the Dads' race when my children were at school, did not mean the end of my football career. However, very early in the 1969/70 season while playing on Greets Green Recreation Ground (known locally as 'The Rec' but more accurately described as 'The Wreck') I sustained a serious injury in what was actually a non-competitive game. The uneven surface of the pitch caused me to turn my ankle very awkwardly and I fell to the ground with no more than a slight pain which prompted the reflex action of my hand going down to 'rub it better'. To my horror I felt the bottom ends of my tibia and fibula through the skin which was all that was keeping foot and leg together, my toes and heel had changed places!

My Uncle Ernest was watching the game and as an accomplished former player himself, he immediately recognised the severity of the problem and what to do about it. He drove me to the local hospital (the same one I think that confined me to nocturnal splints years before) where I was diagnosed as having a Pott's Fracture. I spent a week in hospital during which a brilliant surgeon by the name of Eric Bajal re-connected my foot to my leg with a screw and a piece of wire, both of which remain in place to date.

For the next four decades I assumed that Dr. Pott had been the first surgeon to identify that type of injury and that was why it bore his name. Then Andrew and Clare took us on a guided tour of City of London places that were in various ways connected to the Royal Society. During that tour I learned that Percival Pott was indeed a fine surgeon and that my type of injury had been named after him. However, the detail was somewhat different to that which I had assumed. He personally sustained a broken leg in a fall from his horse but it was his femur that was fractured, not his ankle. The usual treatment for such injuries at that time was for the broken limb to be amputated to prevent gangrene or some such disease resulting in death.

Percival Pott had other ideas and he ordered his colleagues to straighten up and apply splints to the leg instead. In time he made almost a full recovery and lived for many more years during which he led some pioneering work in the field of cancer research. I don't think it unreasonable of me on the basis of these facts to credit him with the fact that Eric Bajal didn't simply amputate my leg that day. However, I do wonder whether or not he also gave Mr Kirkham the idea of using splints to cause me restless nights as a child!

Pott's Fracture

I owe a leg to Percival Pott.

When I was young I hated to walk,
I wanted to run everywhere.
And quite quickly too.
Olympic standard, no less, was the talk,
just for a furlong with breath to spare.

In 1969 my foot broke off,
except for ligaments and skin:
no skeletal support remained.
With bated breath I felt the bones within
and saw my heel misaligned.

By then it was a call for a running repair,
a screw there and a wire here.
Months in plaster meant no walks to bear,
just swinging on crutches, oh dear,
or hopping everywhere.

Two hundred years before that date,
when Doctor Pott broke a thigh,
his colleagues forecast a far worse fate
and prepared to amputate the limb.
If not, he would surely die.

But "Hold!" said he "Put down your blade
and strap my leg to splints"
The femur fused and he walked, with aid,
for the rest of his lengthy life
and gave the future some useful hints.

I owe a leg to Percival Pott

In the 1950s and 1960s, a period during which many of the motorways and dual carriageways of Great Britain were designed and constructed, quantity surveyors and land surveyors handling those types of project grew both in number and importance. However, the qualifying and regulatory bodies to which they belonged had been founded in earlier times, times in which such projects were regarded as part of the building industry or had been dealt with by the Military. The term 'civil engineering' is one intended merely to distinguish it from 'military engineering'. As a consequence, surveyors found that they had to qualify as such by learning skills inappropriate or unrelated to the work they would be doing, or try to build careers without formal qualifications in their specialist field. The situation gave rise to a group of such surveyors forming what became the Chartered Institution of Civil Engineering Surveyors of which I became a student member in 1974, qualified in 1979 and went on to be President in 1997. In 2006 it was announced that the last surviving active member of that founding group was to retire from his post as Executive Director.

He is C. Kevin Blackwell, who was, for many years, as fond of his Florida holiday home as he was of Old Trafford, home of his beloved Manchester United Football Club, whilst remaining faithful to his real home and to the Sale headquarters of the Institution. There is little doubt that he will remain close to the Institution and to the many friends he has made, of which I am proud to be one, on a social basis for many years to come. The date of the announcement of his retirement coincided with the bicentenary of another iconic figure in the world of civil engineering about whom there is more later but whose initials are similar, Isambard Kingdom Brunel.

This one, yet another Shakespearean sonnet, is just for you, Kevin, in return for many years of friendship and for the ticket you bought me to see the first ever Premiership appearance of my team. It was against your team on August 16th 2002 and although we lost 1 − 0 and the referee sent our captain off for a harmless tackle while allowing a certain, notoriously dirty Manchester United player to stay on the field after a far worse offence, I still have the video recording of it, as you will read elsewhere.

Our Kevin

Old Trafford and Florida know his name
but his heart and head are both nearer Sale.
It is hard to sing praise, and not sound lame,
as this man's record makes others look pale.
There to begin with, nay, he WAS the start
of I.C.E.S., home for surveyors galore.
His wit has been felt, like a well aimed dart,
all over the World but, sadly, no more.
At least not as leader, now just our friend:
he will long be with us. There, at the bar!
And nothing will change, it is not the end:
what he has constructed time will not mar.
Two hundred years we had IKB.
For many more yet we'll have CKB.

Throughout the 1970s there was a tendency for British construction workers of all types to seek employment in the Middle East for a few years as a means of earning high wages. Massive building and civil engineering projects funded by Arabian oil were underway and salaries up to four times that paid in the UK were being offered, together with tax-free status and numerous other fringe benefits. I was never interested, although in 1977 I gave serious consideration to a two year contract in Saudi Arabia with the UK company employing me at the time. It was only when I saw an example of the way they dealt with wayward Princesses there that the interest ended. If they can publicly execute a member of their own Royal family there is no way of knowing what they might do to me, I thought, and stayed at home.

However, in 1988 the island of Jamaica was badly damaged by Hurricane Gilbert and for some reason I immediately became keen to go and help with the restoration of the buildings. My then employer agreed and I went to work in Kingston with substantial financial benefits and a chance of adventure. The working conditions were hard but the social life was quite good, spoiled only by repeated bouts of digestive difficulties.

After a few weeks, my good friend and colleague in the UK, Andrew Carleton, joined the team and became my room-mate at the Liguanee Club. For a month we then suffered together and took full advantage of the social scene in the evenings and weekends, Andrew being a natural entertainer and bon viveur. We saw many interesting sights including the prison yard mentioned at the start of Bob Marley's song, *'No woman, no cry'* and, in dealing with several matters of hurricane damage suffered by his widow, Rita, we were called to her house on Skyline Drive. We returned to UK just before Christmas and Andrew did the usual round of parties, entertaining everyone with his hilarious versions of our experiences in the Caribbean, mostly embellished but to great effect. Our friendship had been formed a few years earlier when we were both having certain life problems, mainly shortage of money. However, the Jamaica adventure sealed that friendship which continued to develop into the new millennium.

I wrote *'Carleton came'* early in 1989 but more recently revised the third stanza to reflect one aspect of our later life, Karaoke singing. It could have been invented for us and the early signs of that were the taking over the microphone from a professional singer at a cabaret in Ocho Rios one weekend, the episode upon which the original version was based.

Carleton came

I had no wish to work abroad
when chances came to build there.
So why was I so easily made
to think that I must go where
damaged structures had been brought
to ruin by Gilbert's blowing?
To get away? To have a break?
To pay the money owing?

For weeks I toiled beneath the Sun
and spent each evening drinking.
But every hour I had to run
because my guts were sinking.
Then Carleton came and all was well,
my old mate gave me reason
to do my time and stay the course
until the Christmas Season.

Together at The Liguanee
we never did stop joking,
The Queen of Spades, the Vaseline,
the snooker and the soaking.
The days up North, the ganja man,
the karaoke singing
then back to Kingston and Bob's yard
with Rita's Skyline ringing.

In Birmingham he told those tales,
his audience were in stitches.
And tears of laughter wet my cheeks
with joy beyond all riches.
A bond that formed when we were sad
was stronger with us cheerful.
My friend for life, and then beyond,
of that do not be fearful.

From about 1989 onwards my friendship with Andy Carleton grew from that of workmates who enjoyed a lunchtime drink to that of close friends. In our impoverished past I had once given him an overcoat that, by then, I had owned for no less than twenty years, simply because he didn't have one and I had two. Always a man of fashion, Andy would rather shiver than wear it but he did swap it with one his father, Russell, had and he did, therefore, derive some benefit from my gift.

Twice a year throughout the 1980s, our working colleagues spent an entire Saturday on a coach tour of public houses, alternatively in Dovedale and Shropshire, as young men are wont to do. I had young children at home at that time and always declined offers to join the days out despite Andy regaling me with up-beat accounts of each trip in the pub the following Monday lunchtime. By 1989, I had been converted and joined the trips thereafter, the Shropshire trip always coinciding with the F. A. Cup Final which was watched on TV in the pub at which we took lunch.

Andy's daughter, Ashleigh, was about four years old when I first got to know him and his son, Baillie, was born a year or two later. I became fond of both of them and took enormous pride and pleasure in attending Ashleigh's Wedding Celebrations in 2006. Another daughter, Nicola, was born in 1991 but, temporarily I hope, I have lost touch with her since 2001.

Andy took and passed the examinations of the Chartered Institute of Loss Adjusters and sought my coaching as a Chartered Surveyor when preparing for the paper on Building. He passed it with Distinction and it remained a source of amusement to him that I only achieved a basic pass! Subversive moves were made by some to create a professional situation that, as a by-product not an objective, could have driven a wedge between Andy and I but they did not succeed in either respect.

To my great sadness, Andy died in 2001 after a five year battle against a brain tumour. Our friendship lives on through his family. He was a great admirer of the musician, Sting, to whom he bore a physical resemblance and, as the song that was played at his funeral suggests, he'll be watching us!

It was with a heavy heart that, early in 2002, I wrote *'Now he's gone'* which, as you may by now be able to hazard a guess, is in the style of a Sicilian sonnet.

Now he's gone

A poem to his honour I once wrote
when we were all much brighter than today.
We laughed about when I gave him a coat,
he swapped for one of Russ's, by the way.
The Dovedale trips, and those to Clun as well,
I missed for years until I found my way.
On Monday lunchtimes he would always tell
me what they'd done the previous Saturday.

As years passed by, a family bond we made,
his children, two then three, became mine too.
By training, our foundations were well laid,
despite the tricks of others we'd the glue
to hold the friendship that will never fade.
Death has its Sting but, Andy, we have you.

At the age of five I contracted the childhood disease known as measles. Despite closed curtains to limit my exposure to bright light, the illness left me with a weak left eye. I was prescribed spectacles for reading and writing but I was never convinced that they were actually of any use. Horrible things they were, with hook-shaped springs that wrapped around the ears to secure the apparatus against the energetic excesses of youngsters, I presume. Personally, I have never been that energetic whilst either reading or writing so the technology was superfluous in my case.

By the age of fifteen I was being told that I no longer needed to wear the spectacles but by thirty I was finding that my eyes became tired after a few hours close work and I therefore resumed the practice of wearing spectacles, albeit without the spring loading! This happy situation continued, with a change of equipment every few years and with the lens on the right side being almost plain glass whilst the left increasingly took on the appearance of the bottom of a milk bottle. But then I turned fifty and my right eye joined the list of anatomical parts that were reaching their 'best by date'. It wasn't a major problem at first but it was nevertheless irritating to have to fumble for aid to read a menu, a railway timetable, a football programme to check the name of the opposition full-back who had just fouled one of our men, or to pick up a message on my cell-phone. I remained able to see action on the far side of the pitch or in the further goal mouth from my seat in the East Stand.

Conversely, I was unable to drive a car or even to walk about the house safely whilst wearing my prescribed reading glasses. I was able to conduct building surveys as well (or as badly) as ever except that, when in poor light indoors, I had to use specs to write down my observations. It was deliberate concealment by the operators, not my poor eyesight, that caused my failure on several occasions to spot speed cameras and thereby find myself compelled to make cash contributions to the Home Office. The final straw came on 14th February 2006 when the 'chip and pin' system became standard. For years I had been able to scrawl my signature on credit card slips, knowing that anywhere near the bottom would do. With chip and pin you need to be able to see what the machine is telling you to do at any given moment.

Action was clearly required and I therefore consulted my optician who came up with the idea of a varifocal contact lens. My right eye was still just about good enough to work unaided, provided that the very weak left eye could be encouraged to share the job of seeing. So, until I could become accustomed to using these things, I was given a single small disc of soft, transparent plastic to moisten then apply to the surface of my left eye. When I eventually overcame my natural defence reflexes and managed to insert the lens I could appreciate the theory of its design but, by then, my eye surround was so sore from the effect of inserting it that the beneficial effect was substantially diminished. The next two weeks were a continuous battle, first to install the object and then to suffer the discomfort of its presence. The idea of eventually moving onto a pair was soon abandoned.

Cheap spectacles can be bought at any supermarket or department store and give straightforward magnification. I acquired two matching pairs, one with 1.25X enlargement and the other twice as strong. Using a jewellers' screwdriver, I swapped the lenses to give the stronger lens to my left eye and the weaker one to my right. A great idea but with an adverse effect on my balance and on my judgement of distance, pretty much the same as would a bottle of Courvoisier. Driving would have been both murderous and suicidal. When the problem first started to develop, my optician suggested bifocal spectacles which I did try at the time but without any success. Now, ten years on, the time was right and as I walked from Colin Lee's shop in the centre of Lichfield in a pair of very expensive rimless bifocals, I knew that a compromise between the sharp eyes of my youth and the days, still to come, when stronger measures will be required, had been found.

Unfortunately, I now need less light to be able to see and the flipside of this is that when there is too much light, as I found in the sunshine of Lanzarote on my first bifocal holiday, the dazzle has a negative effect. Conventional sun glasses revert me to 'chip and pin roulette' and my darkened reading glasses make me a menace on the road. It was therefore necessary to acquire a pair of bifocal sunglasses, but the constant need to change them for the others every time the sun went behind one of the many dark clouds that grace the summer skies in this country eventually led me to buy a pair of those clever ones that react to the sunlight by going dark in the sunshine but then automatically going clear again when the cloud comes over. Colin Lee is doing very well out of my ageing eyes!

There had to be a poem and *'Bifocal'* is that bit of fun. It is very heavy on playful alliteration and, as is often the case, I simply could not resist another chance to take a side-swipe at the Blair-Brown partnership although even I struggle to put forward a convincing case against them for either my bad eyes or my speeding fines!

Bifocal

I could find a faulty fascia at fifteen feet
and recognise a ridge tile that was wrong.
I could spot a sagging soffit-board from the street
and describe defective down-pipes, badly hung.

I could witness wizard wing-play on the west side
and scintillating saves at Smethwick End.
I could clock a cash-cow camera in its hide,
built to boost Brown's biggest bounty for his friend.

But putting pen to paper, problems to proclaim,
and reading restaurant reckoning, written small,
might mean mistaken memos. Menus? Much the same
when shifting focus from a fractured wall.

A pair of lick-on lenses looked like working well
but foreign bodies bubble in my eyes.
And simple spectacles, the sort that Sainsbury's sell,
would weaken wide-road vision, most unwise!

So what was one to do with eyes they were so weak?
The answer was, as always, very local.
Whilst perfect peeping probably has passed its peak,
without that it is best to be bifocal

When my interest in 'the beautiful game' started, Stanley Matthews and Tom Finney were still playing, George Best and Willie Johnston were still at school and David Beckham was two decades away from being born. Jimmy Greaves had yet to make his mark on the game and Jeff Astle, Bobby Moore and Geoff Hurst were completely unknown. With the enthusiasm and total thoroughness of learning that only youngsters have, I knew all the top players by name (desperate, incidentally, to find one called Graham) but I could not name a single referee. Former referees such as Arthur Ellis and Stanley Rous became well-known but not as referees, the earliest to achieve notoriety (oh, all right then, fame) being a chap called Ken Aston whom I seem to recall being distinguished from the rest simply because he was good at his job.

Jack Taylor was a close contemporary and was renowned for similar qualities but, in 1974, he was given the World Cup Final to look after. Having given Holland a first minute penalty, he felt the need to balance that up and he awarded another one to their opponents, West Germany, later in the game. Whether or not either or both were correct decisions is entirely immaterial. The effect was that the spotlight was on the referee at least as much as on the two teams that each contained some of the all time greats of football, such as Franz Beckenbauer and Johann Cruyff. Others then saw the chance to achieve what their lack of football talent would always deny them, that is to say media attention and what they still see as fame and glory. Clive Thomas in effect succeeded Jack Taylor as England's leading referee and some of his decisions were truly astonishing but always kept him in the news.

Others yet achieved immortality because of mad decisions, such as Ray Tinkler who allowed my team to score a goal from what every player on the pitch and every supporter in the ground could see was an offside position. This cost Leeds United the game, the league title and a punishment for crowd protest that arguably cost them the title the following season too. These hangers-on used to be given a medal if they handled the FA Cup Final but now get paid salaries that rival doctors. They dress in all colours as well as black and now need fourth and sometimes fifth officials as well as two linesmen that they now call assistant referees. All other major sports use modern technology to decide difficult but important matters and the sooner football does the same and puts referees back where they belong the better. *The Men in the Middle'* sets my thoughts on the matter to blank verse.

The Men in the Middle

Those men in black, their henchmen likewise clad,
are truly fireproof and beyond control.
'He robbed us' was the classic chant of those
who saw it all and knew the rules by heart.
In better days their nameless, faceless form
was rarely seen except in shades of grey.
They knew their place, were grateful for the chance
to sweep the stage where better men had played.
Their part, the most despised on Saturday,
was more or less forgotten in a week
and, once a year, their breed had its big day;
a medal from the Monarch, not a fee.
The taste of power once caused Leeds to miss
their title aspirations, Thank you Ray.
'I'm bigger than you, Don.' He seemed to say,
the offside rule suspended at his whim.
Then, prior to a Welshman causing strife,
the penny dropped that he was not the first
to write his name as large as greater folk
in whose reflected glory he could bathe.
Not just one but two spot kicks were given
to teams with Beckenbauer and with Cruyff.
No bias shown as He took centre stage
and raised the expectations of his ilk.
For many years they stayed in monochrome
and, by and large, did not proliferate
but then the lure of lucre took effect
and show-off referees became the norm.
Just like the peacocks that they emulate
they now come clad in colours, four at once.
We can but hope that science will succeed
and knock them from the pedestals they've built.

It is perhaps apparent from some of my poems and anecdotes that I am not, by nature, a Socialist. After the death of John Smith, leadership of the Labour Party passed to a youthful Tony Blair. Together with henchmen such as Peter Mandelson and Gordon Brown, he converted the anachronistic remains of his party into an electable entity which came to power in May 1997 and remained despite having become a busted flush sometime during its second term until 2010 . Sadly, the Conservative Party has stumbled from one failed leader to another during the same period, searching still for a worthy successor to Margaret Thatcher, and had been unable to put up any worthwhile opposition. In 2007, Blair finally did as he had promised earlier and handed the reins to Gordon Brown. At the height of his potential as one of the great Prime Ministers of all time, which he never did become, he made a big deal of treating education as a priority by his famous 'Education. Education. Education' speech. Unfortunately his ten year sojourn in Downing Street will be remembered for several other things. He soon fell into the trap of believing himself to be omnipotent and developed delusions of adequacy. Filling the void left on the World stage when George W Bush gave up foreign travel after the '9 11' attack, Blair chose to stake his claim for a place in history by declaring war on Iraq, a certain amount of synergy coming from 'Dubya' who, puppet-like, was determined to finish the job his father had started some years before. Blair deceived the British public and Parliament into accepting that Iraq had weapons of mass destruction which could be turned against us in forty five minutes and that this justified the complete disregard of the United Nations. Together they invaded Iraq and remain in occupation of this once-great nation to date. Another hallmark of Blair's reign was the elevation to the Peerage and the award of lesser honours to his buddies, especially the rich ones. Protected as if by a coating of 'Teflon', he escaped all responsibility for those wrongdoings. Part of the art of staying at the top for so long was throwing a scrap to the 'Old Labour' dogs by making John Prescott his Deputy and giving Gordon Brown the job of Chancellor of the Exchequer. With some 'Old Labour' tendencies of his own still lingering, Brown set several time bombs ticking which will explode in the faces of his successors as inflation when the final bills have to be paid. Some shrapnel may strike Brown but Blair will escape completely from this too. Soon after the actual date of his resignation was announced, Blair paid a visit to the Pope. Maybe it was as Head of State rather than as God's man on Earth or maybe it was because he fancies the job himself some day! **'Ten Years at Number Ten'** is another light hearted jibe at Blair's miserable reign of terror but in truth it is no laughing matter, the legacy of that regime is a debt that my grandchildren will still be paying back when they are forty, and they haven't even been born yet.

34

Ten Years at Number Ten

Election. Election. Election.
Education. Education. Education.
Delusion. Delusion. Delusion.
Deception. Deception. Deception.
Invasion. Invasion. Invasion.
Occupation. Occupation. Occupation.
Allegation. Allegation. Allegation.
Inflation. Inflation. Inflation.
Resignation. Resignation. Resignation.
Absolution? Absolution? Absolution?

In the alliance between what remains of our Empire and the temporary and artificial union of sworn enemy states within Europe, I sometimes fear could lie the spark that may yet ignite the war that really will end all wars. Perhaps this spark flickers for now in Turkey or perhaps it is already further West. In my earlier years I formed a certain view which I have reluctantly had to modify in recent years. This was that withdrawal from the European Union was a preliminary condition for the long-term existence of our England other than as a collection of post codes. I have been forced to concede that our glorious past has gone forever and that it is now in our long term interests to stay in the European Union.

However, more recently, I have concluded that Scottish infiltration generally and in particular when combined with the deceptive policies of the Labour Party is destined to bring more and more misfortune to the English nation and that our national feeling is by no means the match for the dynamic patriotism of other nations, including those to which we are officially allied. On the positive side, the first of these recent views may eventually bring about the end of the union with Scotland as, I sincerely believe, would be the majority wish of the good citizens of both nations. To allow only one side to vote on the partial devolution that led to the formation of the Scottish Parliament was disgraceful enough but to allow Scottish Members to remain in the English Parliament afterwards, and moreover to control it, is nothing short of a sick joke to play on those of us who love England. I must be clear in stating that I have every admiration and respect for the Scottish people (with the exception of the football fans who still worship Diego Maradona for the way he cheated England out of the World Cup in 1986) and the massive contributions they have always made to global civilisation but I do not wish to take orders from them any more than they would wish to take orders from us. Those Scots whom I love the best sympathise, if not always fully agree, with me on this point.

It has always been a bit of a mystery to me as to why we, as a nation, have such a long history of putting foreigners on our throne as soon as one dynasty starts to look and feel almost English. After the Germans eventually completed their Anglicisation in 1917 by changing their name to Windsor, it was only a few short years before the heir threw in the towel and married an American, leaving his brother with a Scottish wife ready to take over. The present incumbents have clearly inherited that tartan blood. *'Bannockburn re-visited'* is another tongue-in-cheek poem arising from the more serious comments made above.

Bannockburn re-visited

In days gone by, a wall of stone
from coast to coast sufficed
to keep at bay the Northern drones
and halt the sacrifice
of hard-won progress from the South,
civilisation's bounty,
which blessed the life of every youth,
in every town and county.

When Braveheart made his final stand,
ending hung in quarters,
a winning time enriched our land,
beating all who fought us.

Culloden should have put an end
to Kings above the border,
Germanic rulers could defend
the Faith, the Law, the Order.

And then, like Campbells in Glencoe,
they came to rule by creeping
into the Monarch's bed and so
English power went seeping
into a pit, lost for all time,
whilst tartan armies flourished
and set in train a dreadful crime,
their egos never nourished.

Since the beginning of the 20th century we have been going backwards as a World power although we have so far been able to maintain a top ten place, largely because of our so-called 'special relationship' with the USA which was the first Nation to take over our top spot, and which has stayed there ever since. This relationship is a symbiotic one in that our reputation and glorious history lends to the USA an air of antiquity and respectability whilst the sheer size and wealth of the USA lends to us a feeling and indeed, for now, a reality of security – we shall not be conquered, at least not in combat, whilst the USA is on our side. The price we have to pay is that we are expected to give our avuncular blessing to this bully as he insults, invades, threatens and generally torments weaker nations.

Perhaps it is unfair to dismiss all of this international interference as simply bullying, although the USA has certainly seen itself as a World Policeman for many years. Underlying the perceived right, perhaps even a perceived duty, that the USA arrogates onto itself to ensure as far as it dares that the governments, laws and customs of all other nations are acceptable, it does have a thinly veiled fear that it will eventually run out of oil and oil suppliers. This is the main reason for the interference. The American peoples are devoted to the internal combustion engine and to as many other forms of using up Earth's resources that they can think of. When, as does happen from time to time, a nation rises that not only has oil supplies but also has a leader or government that is possibly corrupt or simply wasn't democratically elected, then in goes the USA with guns being fired from the hip, with the British Army dragged along as cannon fodder, spear carriers or, it seems frequently, as target practice for 'friendly fire'.

Personally, I am of the view that it is none of my business nor anyone else's what goes on within the boundaries of a foreign country. When they are positioned within range of our borders and look well-armed and threatening then we should react, and react as forcibly as we can, such as in The Falklands in 1982: yes, the Falklands ARE within our borders because the people who live there want them to be, not because we want their sheep! Until then, foreigners are as entitled as we are to run their own countries as they see fit without our interference. At any given moment there are numerous nations within which things are not being run the way we would want to run our own but we are being allowed by the USA to stay out.

However, when there is the chance of gaining some oil, or perhaps of not losing out on some already accounted for, it is never long before those nations get invaded by the USA and the leaders are deposed. Simultaneously, anyone with enough money can become President of the USA, especially if they have a relative or two already in a position of influence. Democracy, as the USA knows it, is the best system of government that money can buy! The USA has never fully recovered from the ridiculous 'reds under the beds' fiasco in the wake of World War II when hundreds of perfectly honest and loyal citizens were chastised and ostracised in a witch hunt started or at least led by Joseph McCarthy to root out communists. Considering the fact that the USA had spent a few years in the early 1940s helping the British, the Russians and, to some extent, the French to defeat the strongest anti-Communist force on Earth, therefore being tenuous Allies to communists, bear in mind, it represents a serious *volte face* in my view and displays the inconsistency of the American thinking which continues to date. It is odd that a nation made up of such a broad range of genetically different peoples should have such a commonality of thinking. But do they really have this consensus?

It will be interesting to see where they stand as a nation on this point in thirty or forty years time, although I very much doubt that I shall personally see it.

At the time of writing, the old McCarthy claptrap is still there and rises to the fore at every opportunity. Fortunately, since the Bay of Pigs scare there has been nothing more dangerous than throwing the rattle out of the pram at the time of the 1980 Olympics. This was not an official Olympic event, you understand, just a figure of speech to describe the trivial and churlish attitude of both USA and our own government to what I regard as the border dispute between USSR and Afghanistan. It was of course considered to be perfectly acceptable for the same country to be invaded by a USA/UK combined force a few years later.

Since 1980, the USSR has been disbanded and it has become clear that there is a lot of oil in those parts. The temptation of having a militarily weakened enemy which has vast energy resources will, I fear, become too great for the USA to resist and a reason will be found and inflicted upon the toothless United Nations Organisation for battle to commence. That should quickly lead to the reformation of the USSR but where will it leave us, I wonder. A complex mess if ever there was one but it has been coming for a century or more so we should have worked it out by now. However, circumstances do change and solving the problems is like trying to hit a moving target. The pages of history are covered with the names of those who saw these problems and thought they had the answers to them. Many have tried, some have nearly succeeded and have still been condemned for their efforts. The history of war is always written by the winners, and the losers are never portrayed in a favourable light. I have no idea what the answers are unless we are ever able to persuade all the nations on Earth to stay permanently within their own boundaries and to leave everyone else alone except for mutually beneficial trade. Such a multi-Utopian solution falls at the first hurdle as, after centuries of alternating war and diplomacy, we still cannot even agree with each other as to where those boundaries lie in the first place.

In recent years, two of the components of the former USSR, Russia and Georgia, have been at each others' throats over a boundary dispute and, guess what, Uncle Sam was there egging them on whilst our leaders acted as seconds!

My sincere wish is that the fears expressed in the next poem, which was written in July 2008, never come true but as I wrote it, it was becoming increasingly apparent that George W Bush was spoiling for a fight with Russia. He was to be out of office soon and, impossible as it may have sounded at the time, I thought that worse was to follow him. I just hoped that he was not hell-bent on making another ugly mark on history by starting yet another war, potentially the BIG one, before he left.

Against all the odds, it transpired that the American people were eventually faced with a choice of President taken from a group which included two women, a fragile old man and a guy of African origins with an Islamic middle name. Time alone will tell whether they were right or wrong in appointing the latter but, if they were wrong, it will be because of his arrogant but impotent ways and policies rather than because of his background. I have always assumed that if I were American I would be a Republican but, in the 2008 election, I would have selected Hillary Clinton out of the front–runners so I was both pleased and somehow re-assured by her appointment as Secretary of State

In *'Uncle Oli'* most of the characters will be easy to identify but there is one that you may have to think about for a while.

Uncle Oli

Uncle Oli is smooth and dark
and moves easily when he is out.
Refined, he helps others to move too.
His mother is the Earth herself,
he is a true son of Nature.

Uncle Sam is strong and rich
and moves slowly but sometimes far.
With visits to the sisters of Mother Earth.
He is not a natural child but comes
from an enormous gene pool.

Uncle Sam is in love with Uncle Oli
who, he believes, needs him too.
But Uncle Oli lives with Uncle Ali.
Perverse, perhaps, but not incestuous
as they are related only by spilt blood.

From time to time Uncle Ali checks
Uncle Sam's advances to Uncle Oli.
Out of envy, spite or fear.
This makes Uncle Sam angry and
he is very dangerous and deceitful then.

Uncle Bob is a wicked, evil man
and genetically remote from the others.
Uncle Bob hardly knows Uncle Oli.
So Uncle Sam leaves him alone
to abuse his own family as he will.

Uncle Ivan also has Uncle Oli at home
and loves him too, like a brother.
Uncle Sam despises Uncle Ivan.
One day, he may take Uncle Oli from him
and then the sparks will fly!

In the following poem I draw heavily upon paraphrasing the works of William Shakespeare. I have never been an ardent admirer of his plays as for me most of them have zero entertainment value in their original form although I must say that I thoroughly enjoyed Franco Zeffirelli's film of *'Romeo and Juliet'* when I saw it a few years ago. I had also enjoyed it the first time I saw it forty years earlier but that was because I fancied Olivia Hussey who played Juliet. In a similar way, I enjoyed seeing *'Midsummer Night's Dream'* but only because of Diana Rigg

However, as well as inventing a form of sonnet that I use frequently, Shakespeare did have a good turn of phrase and I am indebted to him for several lines in *'Blair, Brown and the Bard'*. I think most of the 'misquotes', which include titles as well as lines from several plays will be easy to spot but for those of you who like a bit of fun, there are twenty intended allusions to the work of Shakespeare as well as, believe it or not, a few totally original lines of my own! Some of the allusions are obscure and none are intended to be offensive, except to Blair and Brown of course, and the first of two from *'Julius Caesar'* may be hard to spot.

Harold Wilson once said that a week in politics is a long time. As I edit these pages I become increasingly aware that two years in politics is a lifetime for some. For this reason I think I should make it clear that the David I refer to in the final stanza was not Mr Cameron, the man who actually replaced Brown as Prime Minister, but Mr Miliband who was the man who sought to replace Brown first as Prime Minister and then, later, simply as leader of the Labour Party. Until the new government is able to get the country back on its financial feet we have to be grateful for small mercies. Given the fact that after his little brother pulled a fast one on him to steal the Labour crown in a way that would have sent Shakespeare into raptures had they been medieval princes he immediately threw a hissy fit and walked off into the sunset, we as a nation should be relieved that he never did become Prime Minister, well at least not yet. I ranted against the Labour Government for eleven of their thirteen years in power, having given them a fair chance at the beginning of their regime, so I need some new objects of hatred to revile. These may come from the whinging fat cats and idlers who will both have to find a difference in their income soon if the national debt is to be reduced even slightly in the foreseeable future but for the time being it will have to be the unions so watch this space.........................

Blair, Brown and the Bard

A midsummer nightmare came to life
as Teflon Tony slid aside
to make room for the Scottish Player
needing more power, for his pride.

Blair by any name is just as foul,
with England's treasures now in hock,
and Brown still boasting of prudency,
as constant as the Northern Rock.

Throughout the tragedy of errors,
as we go curséd to our beds,
first one then t'other spouting witless
doctrines that grow in empty heads.

Shall he, on the other bench, regain
that fleeting love that Labour lost?
Or, by having far more hair than wit,
could exhumed good reduce the cost?

But curséd is he that moves those bones,
the badge of Hell is always black,
and pampered maids of Asia pick us
clean of sovereigns, sack by sack.

Alas! Poor Gordon knows so well
how David damns him with faint praise
and threatens too, the unkindest cut,
to take his crown in glorious blaze.

Long before I came to live in the tiny city of Lichfield I was extremely fond of it as a place to visit. We passed through it on childhood trips to relatives in Derby and on occasions attended the Whitsuntide carnival that through the ages has been called 'The Bower'. By the 1980s, I had migrated as far East as Sutton Coldfield and was happy to travel a few miles further East to spend a Sunday afternoon, now and then, looking at the beautiful and uniquely three-spired cathedral founded by Saint Chad. The walls are adorned with statues of the Medieval Kings of England and of the Saints, including Chad. The spires, visible from miles around, are often known as the Ladies of the Vale. To the South of the cathedral, leading to the oldest part of the city, around the market place adjacent to the Guild Church of Saint Mary, is Dam Street.

After the cathedral itself, Lichfield is probably best known as the birthplace of Dr. Samuel Johnson. Streets and public houses are named after him, there is a statue of him and his biographer, Boswell, in the aforementioned market place and it is almost impossible to walk for two minutes inside the city boundary without seeing either his image or some other reference to him. What is the measure of reflected glory needed for a statue to be erected to the mere biographer of a great man? Boswell's work was of course of the highest standard but it is doubtful that he would have been commemorated as the biographer of anyone else. Friends of Johnson have shops and restaurants named after them and, on Dam Street there is Dame Oliver's house, as well as a shop named after her, in which she taught the young Samuel Johnson.

That is the backdrop to the *'Ballard of the Three Spires'*. I wanted to write a poem in praise of the place in general and the cathedral in particular and the inspiration finally came from the most unlikely of sources. First World War poet, Ivor Gurney, wrote a piece called the *'Ballad of the Three Spectres'* which I read one day and instantly had the title and theme for my poem. However, an unexpected bonus came from Gurney's opening line *'As I went up by Ovillers'*. An Anglicised pronunciation of the battle zone town in France sounds a lot like *'Oliver's'* and this gave me my own first line.

44

Ballad of the Three Spires

As I went past Dame Oliver's
on Dam Street, heading North,
in front of me there were three spires
who said "What is our worth?"

The South West one spoke through the moss.
"Our task is known to all!
We each support a golden cross,
without us they would fall"

"Well maybe so," her sister said,
"but surely there is more.
We point to where the Saints have led:
those Saints above the door"

The other spire spoke from the East.
"You're both right, friends, but wait.
Admiring eyes upon us feast:
not on Saint Peter's Gate"

Those Ladies of the Vale do me,
with all their charms, ensnare.
They need no task, for all can see
them standing, ever fair.

2006 was the 250th anniversary of the birth of Wolfgang Amadeus Mozart, the composer, of whom I have been a great admirer since 1971 when his work was drawn to my attention by the popularisation of part of his 40th Symphony by Waldo de los Rios. Partly for this reason, Denise and I decided to visit the region of his birth as part of a summer holiday. Rather than stay in Salzburg itself, although we did visit the Birthplace and other worthy sights, we stayed in the small town of St. Wolfgang, a few miles away and one of several towns and villages on the shores of a lake known as Wolfgangsee.

The general area is called Salzkammergut. The lake is overlooked by a mountain which, from some angles, has the look of a couchant lion. In the summer of 2007, in the footsteps of Wordsworth, I visited the lakes of Italy. However, Wolfgangsee and its surroundings remain the most serenely beautiful of the many places on Earth that I have had the good fortune to visit. Another favourite place of mine, not particularly beautiful nor serene but delightful in other ways, is the town of Lagos in Portugal's Algarve. It has a church dedicated to the legend of a young man who, in temper, kicked his mother then, beside himself with remorse, removed the offending foot with an axe. An obliging local saint caused it to grow back and the rest, whilst not as they say being history, is a decent tale nonetheless.

Saint Wolfgang has a similar tale to tell. Wolfgang, after whom the musician was indirectly named by his mother, was a recluse of the first order. He lived in a cave up in the mountains and was in perpetual fear of Satan creeping up behind him and throwing him from his mountain lair into the lake. At last Wolfgang received Divine inspiration. He was to throw his axe as far as he could and, on the spot where it landed, he was to build a church. Successful completion of these tasks would guarantee eternal protection from Satan's threat. As luck would have it, in those days before coffer dams and underwater piling technology, the axe cleared the lake and landed on good ground where the church now stands. Outside is a statue of the canonised Wolfgang holding his axe and gazing avuncularly on the lovely, lovely people of the town named after him and the equally lovely buildings in which they are fortunate enough to live and work.

I hope they will forgive my teasing in this poem which I wrote while soaking in the bath in our room at Hotel Furian.

Salzkammergut

Lion Mountain lying,
proud but with no pride.
Singing breezes mingling
with birdsong at the side
of waters lapping at the shores,
from Strobl to St. Gilgen,
in time with music from the scores
by Mozart, sent from heaven.

Caring townsfolk sharing
their fayre with all who come.
Rendered houses tended
by those who are at home
in these small towns that draw us
from everywhere on Earth
to gaze like those before us.
Hear our joyous mirth!

Be-devilled hermit levelled
the land to build a church.
God-guided axe decided where
when thrown from lofty perch.
His wooden effigy now guards
the market place, the fountain
and sloping roofs with jerkin heads
in the shadow of his mountain.

During the visit to Salzkammergut, we had intended to make a day trip to Vienna. However, this proved to be too ambitious as an eighteen hour round trip from St. Wolfgang to Vienna via Salzburg would leave insufficient time to see more than a tiny fraction of what Vienna has to offer. As soon as we returned to England, therefore, we made arrangements to spend a few days in Vienna and we were fortunate enough to be joined on that adventure by my wonderful cousin Maureen and her husband Steve Potter. Staying, ironically, in the Hotel Beethoven, we toured Royal Palaces, Museums and Art Galleries. We stood and stared in awe at the Opera House and countless other buildings equally impressive and sampled the delights of a Mozart concert at the Hofburg as well as the wurst and torte at the Hotel Sacher. Unlike many major cities, Vienna was scrupulously clean and its people polite, friendly, helpful and inviting. They say that there is almost no crime in Vienna and, although they would say that to tourists, wouldn't they, I do believe them. So is this Utopia? Has this city, that has been central to key historical events for centuries also achieved a state of perfection? Sadly, the answer is 'No!'. The people seem to share a habit of continuously smoking the foulest smelling cigarettes outside France. There are no apparent legal rules or social disapprovals to restrain them and the exquisite flavour of many a bowl of goulash was impaired by a smoker sitting nearby.

Back home, in the clean air of Staffordshire, I wrote **'Rauchen Verboten'** using a very large proportion of my total German vocabulary. Curiously, I wrote this in half an hour in German rather than in English to be translated later. In some cases the forty years passage of time since my last German lesson had served to diminish my always tenuous grasp of grammatically correct word endings but, there again, that applies to my English too! The first part is addressed to the people of Vienna and the second to Vienna itself. At the end of the second line of the second stanza I used the word 'fuhrer'. I did this for two reasons. First, I recalled it as being the German word for 'leader' and, second, I wanted to say that the city and its people deserve the title that was taken for his own by that evil madman, Adolf Hitler. In checking and correcting my grammar, my old friend Dr. Gillian James suggested that I substitute a word I had never previously encountered, 'leiter'. Not only did this substitution remove any possibility of my poem unintentionally offending the very people I sought to extol but it also provided a useful half-rhyme with 'leute'. Thank you, Gill, for that and other improvements to my draft. Both **'Rauchen verboten'** and its translation to English follow.

Rauchen verboten!

Rauchen nicht, meine wunderbare Leute
Ihr seid meine Freunde und meine Helden.
Eure Gebäude und Eure Kunst sind schon
Eure Geschichte und Eure Musik haben keine Überstehenden
O, Wien, ich liebe Dich und Deine Leute
Du bist meine Geliebte und unser Leiter
Deine Kinder sind meine Schwestern
und meine Brüder, ich will Euch immer lieben
Rauchet nicht sondern für immer leben!

Smoking is forbidden!

Do not smoke my wonderful people
You are my friends and my heroes
Your buildings and your art are beautiful
Your history and your music have no superior
Oh Vienna, I love you and your people
You are my beloved and our leader
Your children are my sisters
and my brothers, I will always love you.
Do not smoke but live forever!

Sometimes poems seem to write themselves as if freed, like the Genie of the Lamp, by the gentle rubbing of my pen between thumb and forefinger.

Early in 2006, Denise and I were staying with Robert and Angela Rawsthorn at Afton Lodge where they lived, on the outskirts of Freshwater, Isle of Wight. The upper floors at Afton Lodge give amazing views of Tennyson Down from beyond the Monument to the distant ridge over Freshwater Bay and the Military Road. One evening we watched spellbound as thousands of rooks made continuously changing shapes in the fading light for what seemed like an hour before roosting in the nearby trees. Liz Rawsthorn, visiting her parents and us, thoughtfully provided us with the knowledge that one of the collective names for rooks is 'a building'. I must confess that I had thought that these were starlings until I was corrected by my friends.

Awake at dawn the following day, I was somehow reminded that it was the 200th anniversary of the birth of the great engineer, Isambard Kingdom Brunel. For me, Brunel is a contender, behind Isaac Newton, for the title of 'Greatest Ever Englishman'. One of the many reasons for my admiration is the fact that he managed to align the tunnel under Box Hill, Wiltshire in such a way that the rising sun shines through it from end to end every year on his birthday, 9th April. The Heel Stone at Stonehenge boasts a similar success at mid-summer but the sheer showmanship of Brunel in doing it for his own birthday sets him apart from the anonymous Druid (or was it an Ancient Egyptian?) who first came up with the idea of this type of link between building and Nature. Not limited to tunnels, Brunel also conquered the seas with huge metal ships such as S.S. Great Britain and designed marvellous bridges such as the one across Clifton Gorge, near Bristol. The Latin inscription in St. Paul's Cathedral in London declares it to be the monument to its designer, Sir Christopher Wren. I think of Brunel's work as performing a similar job for him. Later the same morning I made the short journey to The Needles and to Freshwater Bay, as I never tire of seeing the rock formations. For many years Freshwater Bay was symbolised by a rock that had eroded to form an arch but this eventually collapsed in the 1990s, leaving just two which are known locally as Mermaid and Stag. These sights completed my poem *'Monuments'* by giving it a spiritual feel which I think is as close as I am ever likely to get to the wonderful *'Paradox'* by Tina Negus. Unusually for me, it is written in free verse but that is not to say that the use of words is entirely random, there are some rhymes and chimes.

Monuments

The ninth day of April, two thousand and six
Anno Domini, they used to say,
and I am early awake with the rising sun
through an unshaded window, reflecting.
Left bare to maintain my view of Tennyson Down,
foreshortened slumber a small price to pay for this sight:
little compares with this growing light.
The dawn chorus further stimulates my waking senses as did
the roosting of the rooks at the previous dusk,
a building of rooks some say.
This Afton is as sweet as any other, I think.
The top of Alfred's monument can just be seen, glistering
and that stirs my senses of history.
It is two hundred years since Brunel was born and,
as I muse, the same sun will shine
through one of the many monuments to that engineer:
all of his own building and design.
I speak of the tunnel 'neath Box
and the perfection of its creation which,
along with the ships and the spans,
makes a shrine this day for that man.
Then I rise and see the chalk ridge and the rocks,
Mermaid, Stag and Needles since Arch is no more,
and I picture Clifton Gorge and that hill and the mighty seas.
Are these all monuments, self-built, to Him?
I wonder.
Sometimes I just have to wonder.

After nearly 25 years of membership of the Chartered Institution of Civil Engineering Surveyors, it became 'Buggins' turn' and I was elected President for the year 1997/98. I had been an active member spasmodically during those years but the jury is still out as to whether I was given the honour because they thought I deserved it or because they needed to fill a gap until a better candidate was free. Either way, it was an interesting year although it came and went with me being frustrated in my thwarted attempts to alter certain things in sea-change proportions. The lesson I learned by the experience was that the art of subtle persuasion rather than dynamic leadership is the way to make things happen. The year was not without its high spots and humorous incidents, one of these occurring one Sunday morning when Denise was telling her mother that we were going to Hong Kong for a while. In an attempt to explain why, she came out with the immortal expression 'Graham isn't just President in this country, he is President of the World'. It became a catch–phrase and gave me a private sense of superiority over US President Bill Clinton when he visited the Midlands during our co-incident terms of office! Hong Kong was most enjoyable and we were among the last to fly into Kai Tak airport with its notorious 90 degree approach turn during which we seemed to be weaving between high rise apartment blocks in which we could see the occupants waving at us. The tour we did of the almost complete but not yet open Chep Lap Kok airport, including a drive down the runway, was also a rare treat. It has become a tradition for Institution Presidents to visit Professor Chen at Shenzhen School of Surveying, to exchange views on the profession and to show support for the many Chinese members of the Institution. We are always well looked after by Professor Chen and his colleagues but it does involve a trip up into Mainland China from Kow Loon. The journey on the Mass Transit Railway could not fail to make one wonder how they can be so clean, efficient and punctual whilst transporting much larger numbers of passengers than their UK counterparts. In many restaurants that we visited, pictures of the recently departed last Governor of Hong Kong, Chris Patten, still hung on the walls. It was clear that the ex-pat community still had a Colonial mentality with every intention of sending their children back to Blighty for schooling, most retaining homes there as possible future bolt-holes. A certain mind-set is needed to live and work abroad and I wondered, in the event that these people had to leave Hong Kong as it became re-absorbed into China, whether they would be able to settle back home. Perhaps they would have to find 'new territories' elsewhere. *'East is West'* is a simple form poem telling the tale light-heartedly but under a serious title that draws attention to the differences and the similarities between life in England and the colonial style, both of which are changing rapidly.

East is West

I went to China for the day,
a feat that may sound strange
for one who lives in Staffordshire,
with flying to arrange.

Shenzhen is further than Shenstone,
you'd say and you'd be right,
but when you start from Hong Kong town
you do not need a flight.

Mass Transit is the way to go,
from Kow Loon to Shenzhen,
it leaves on time, you have a seat,
not herded in a pen.

To meet Professor Chen was fun,
he must be tired of us,
as year by year we visit him,
he always makes a fuss.

A Malta with Manhattan mix,
is what I called Hong Kong,
a 'must-see' once or twice, perhaps,
if you can stand the throng.

We hired it for a hundred years,
before they took it back,
now better placed to lose our rent,
we'd set them on their track.

Presidents come and Gov'nors go,
Chris Patten was the last,
What will become of Hong Kong now,
will ex-pats be out cast?

When they return to Solihull,
to Wilmslow or to Slough,
will they still think their life is full,
or need another, now?

The English Lake District continues to fill me with mixed feelings. For me, it is in a league above Cornwall, the Peak District and the Yorkshire Dales as far as scenery is concerned although at least Cornwall does have the sea. At the same time, it is a poor relation of equivalent regions throughout Europe and North America. I even include the Scottish Lochs in the latter category as another beauty of the Scottish landscape, as opposed to its odious politicians, is that it stays where it belongs!

On separate visits to Windermere, Grasmere, Coniston, Rydal Water and such, I have been disappointed one minute and awe-struck the next: maybe that is why the region is, and has been for two centuries, so popular. I suspect that the connection with William Wordsworth and his friends has also helped the tourist industry more than a little.

It was on one of my more inspired days during a stay at Grasmere's Red Lion Hotel that *'Lakeland Spring'* was written. It is not only about Grasmere but also about neighbouring towns, hills and lakes, as well as taking into account the paths and tracks that link them. Those circular section chimney stacks that abound in the region are charming and seem to soften the otherwise hard edges of the local architecture. From some angles the diminishing courses of the tiled roofs can have the effect of blending in the ridge lines of the buildings to the hills beyond. Harmony with Nature, unbeatable! There is absolutely no need to explain any further the physical features, man-made as well as natural, that are referred to in these blank verses.

What is interesting is that, as with *'Monuments'*, a sort of spiritual theme forces its way into the last few lines. I have no idea who wrote the Christmas song *'I saw three ships'* and I am fairly sure that no-one else does either. However, I am grateful to Graham Hancock for the phrase 'heaven's mirror', although the one he referred to in his book of the same name is in Egypt, about fifteen hundred miles to the East of mine and much drier.

'Lakeland Spring' has proved to be a very popular poem and has been published twice more in poetry magazines since it was first included in *'Across my World'*.

Lakeland Spring

Snow covered hill-tops catch the Sun of Spring,
first give the nether-bracken, brown and mauve,
the iridescence of a starling's chest
then the lived-in look of a threadbare rug.

Walls of rough-cut stone mark the rising banks
like laughter-lines upon a frowning face.
They doubtless have another purpose too;
perhaps to separate the flocks of sheep.

Slated roofs in diminishing courses
surmount the sturdy walls of clean-hewn stone,
are drained by dated gutters of cast-iron
and to round, smokeless chimneys are lead-flashed.

And now the morning mists appear in layers,
some glowing bright as fibre-optic ends,
but some still dull, awaiting random rays
of sun through clouds that cloak the entire scene.

Sombre and naked hollow trees survive
another season, leafless but alive
and soon shall show another coat of green
to complement the eager daffodils.

Icy puddles crackle beneath the feet
that walk in wonder down the coffin path
with startled, grey-fleeced sheep, their faces black,
their eyes, reflective green, like those of cats.

Translucent waves conceal the paddles of
the easy glide of swans upon the lake,
advancing backwards in the forceful flow.
It matters not, there is nowhere to go.

The cob and pen and cygnet sail on by
like those three ships upon a Christmas morn.
And who do we think could have made such ships,
is this, on calmer days, like Heaven's mirror?

One of my great passions in life has been the consumption of sometimes astonishing quantities of red wine, particularly the many varieties from Australia. These are too strong, really, so I tend to stay with the French ones. That said, my drinking achievements in recent years have been very modest indeed and, since I succumbed to the combined effects of old age and family history and suffered a heart attack, my intake has been halved again to make allowance for the medication that thins my blood. Although the wine from Bardolino is not among my favourites, I have been known to sample it on more than one occasion.

During a trip to Italy's Lake Garda I called in at Bardolino and so, unfortunately for me, did thousands of others to crowd the many shops, bars and restaurants. The lake provides a tolerable view to gaze upon over a leisurely lunch – there is no option about it being leisurely as the waiters are the slowest outside Jamaica – except that from many restaurants the views are obscured by lines of people jockeying for position before the next ferry comes in. Not the English, of course, we form orderly queues and sometimes miss the boat as a result! All the time in that part of the World, ear drums are threatened by high-revving but very small capacity motor cycles and scooters. I wonder if I was such a nuisance as I buzzed around on my Vespa in the 1960s; I didn't know then that vespa is Italian for wasp!

The highlight of the town for me was actually the war memorial which comprises a granite obelisk engraved with the names of local men who died in the World Wars of the twentieth century, surrounded at its base by a heavy steel chain supported at each corner by large shell cases positioned like the lions in Trafalgar Square. Italy, of course, entered both of the World Wars of the twentieth century relatively late. Nowhere near as late as the Americans were but certainly later than the 'regulars' like England, Germany and Austria. To the Italians the World Wars were dated 1915 –18 and 1940-45. To embellish the obelisk further are the figures of two men looking less like modern warriors than they do ancient combatants. Or is one simply supporting a fallen colleague?

Either way it is a dramatic sculpture and in the hand of the surviving fighter is what appears to be the gladius of his ancestors with which he is engraving Owen's (or Horace's) 'old lie' Pro Patria............ I was moved to write a short sonnet sequence which I have called simply *'Bardolino I and II'*.

Bardolino I

In Bardolino there is more than wine
to entertain the tourists for a day:
a thousand bars and restaurants form a line,
as well as shops galore, to make them pay.
Before they came, the lake was there for years,
with distant mountains adding to the view.
Now peace is shattered by the screech of gears,
the vista hidden by the ferry queue
But near the town there is a monument
to men from S.Alberti to Zanetti
It covers both the wars where they were sent
to die with Andreoli and Zucchelli.
It seems the townsfolk are, like us, content
to let their men die, alphabetically

Bardolino II

A granite obelisk with rocket fins
stands at the lakeside on the edge of town
A million tourists neither smile nor frown
as war is war, whichever nation wins.
Around the base, an anchor chain is borne
By timeless, nameless shells which, set four-square,
sit like Nelson's lions around his lair.
His triumph once was lauded as a dawn
The start and finish dates of both World Wars
are closer here than by that other lake.
Still time enough to lose men to a cause,
in Latin stated 'for their country's sake'.
Victor and vanquished disobey time's laws
but use a gladius 'the lie' to make.

Living as I do in land-locked Lichfield, for me to get to Garda it was necessary to take a short flight to Verona from Birmingham and then a bus ride of about twenty miles during which I was able to see at least some of the city which I understand was largely made famous by William Shakespeare. I am not a great fan of the Bard although I concede that he was rather more than the 'over-rated medieval scribbler' that I once described him as being to my stunned luncheon colleagues at the Rotary Club in Lichfield.

At one 'Parents' Evening' some years ago, my daughter's English teacher clearly didn't share my opinion either and very politely filed me away mentally under 'Philistine'. I understand that a couple of his plays, including 'Romeo and Juliet' were set in Verona and I have no doubt that the enterprising locals charge handsomely to see the balcony from which Miss Capulet made her speech, whether or not there ever was such a balcony or, for that matter, a Miss Capulet.

What I saw was row upon row of apartment blocks, each with row upon row of elevated walkways at every level, each comprising concrete decks and simple steel parapet fences, unlike the ornately carved stonework that one envisages as supporting the balcony above Master Montague's young and expectant head. I have no idea who the 'two gentlemen' were, nor where they lived and in what arrangement of relationship.

The streets through which we drove were remarkably clean and tidy, with freshly painted buildings down each side, all roofed in what I know as Roman tiles. As this particular fragment of learning came to me at college in England I should not have been surprised to see such tiles in Verona as well, both having been part of the Roman Empire. My intention was to return to Verona for a day during my visit to the region but I didn't find the time and so I must arrange another visit one day.

Who knows, perhaps such a visit would inspire even me to write a play set on its streets and concrete walkways Until then, yet another sonnet, deliberately not in Shakespearean style, will have to sum up my brief encounter with **'Verona'**.

Verona

In Verona many a scene is set.
Fact or fiction? I neither know nor care.
There are a thousand balconies but yet
not one deserving of a maiden, fair.
The well-swept streets with buildings are twice lined,
clean and painted, like an exhibition,
and roofed with Roman tiles, how odd to find
these so far North. But, perhaps, tradition
gives them the name from Empire days, long gone,
ere Garibaldi gave us Italy
and several kings a throne to sit upon
before the fall of that brief monarchy.
My visit here was briefer still, soon gone.
I shall return to learn its history

'New Jersey' was written one afternoon in Lyndhurst, New Jersey, when I should have been writing something much more cerebral. Sometime in the early 1990s, after years of managing construction projects, I enrolled, for reasons long since forgotten if ever known, on a post-graduate course in Construction Project Management. In turn, this led me to spend a couple of weeks which included my forty third birthday studying American techniques in Manhattan. Also for unknown reasons, we actually stayed in Lyndhurst, commuting to New York for meetings and site visits whilst attending lectures and performing various tasks and assignments back at the hotel. A small group comprising Roger Pearce, Mary Morrisey, Adam Westwood and I arrived a few days before the rest and left a day or so after they did. This extra time gave us the opportunity to see the sights to the extent that they could stimulate our interest and it is with enduring regret that although this did include the exteriors of the World Trade Centre and the Empire State Building, we did not, and now never shall in the case of the former, go inside. At least not to the upper floors. Less than a decade later, the 'Twin Towers' had gone! We took pleasure in buying gifts for those at home from the famous Macey's department store, except for Roger who scored his 'Brownie Points' at a discount by buying stuff cheap then putting it in a Macey's bag that he retrieved from a 'trash can'. At the time I thought it odd that Macey's made a ten cent charge for a bag to put purchases from their own store in but maybe it was a rare case of the Americans being ahead of us in the 'save the planet' quest as since then even noble establishments such as Marks and Spencer have started doing the same at home. The question as to why the Empire State Building was so-called arose one day, as it had been built in the 1920s when **the** Empire was already on its last legs and as New York had never been part of it anyway. Most American States have nicknames such as 'garden' 'sunshine' and 'lone star' so we assumed (correctly as it happens) that New York is the Empire State. I vaguely recalled from a cigarette packet nearly thirty years earlier that New York was previously called New Amsterdam and so maybe the name was connected with the Dutch Empire. Nonsense of course but it occupied us until we reached the disappointingly unremarkable Wall Street from the top corner of which we gazed in awe of the 'Twin Towers' and tried hard to capture the scene on camera. Mary, a good Irish Roman Catholic girl from Birmingham, was more interested in acquiring a picture of Saint Patrick's Cathedral for her mother. Throughout our stay, only Adam from our group gave the course the attention it deserved. For most of us it was a holiday, paid for but earned only in part by a few days' study. After two 'Italian jobs' we go back to the Shakespearean sonnet form for this one.

New Jersey

I'm forty three but feeling half of that
here in New Jersey in the Summertime.
We went to Macey's shop, named on the mat
and on the bags, for which they charge a dime.
But Roger bought his bargains on the Mall
and, from the trash can by the deli bar,
he took a wrapper. Yes, he had the gall,
to stow in it a cheapskate perfume jar!
"Why *Empire State*?" remained a mystery
as on to Wall Street and those Towers we walked.
I wondered if it came from Dutch history
but only of Saint Patrick's, Mary talked.
My room-mate, Adam, faithful to the course
that took us there, the rest had no remorse.

The 2006 trip to the Isle of Wight from which *'Monuments'* emerged will also be remembered for the events of one afternoon a few miles inland.

Apart from her poetry and painting, Tina Negus is also a keen photographer with a special interest in church architecture or, more specifically, church embellishments. When she heard that I was to visit the Island she asked me to pop along to the church at Shalfleet and take a photograph for her of the entrance door. It was not the door itself that particularly interested her but the carving on what I would have lazily called the fanlight above it. Actually, it is a tympanum although I have used a bit of licence in the poem that follows and referred to it as an arch, for reasons which will be apparent. In truth, it is the bit between the arch and the horizontal head of the door. Anyway, this particular tympanum is of stone and is carved to display a male figure with a couple of generic animals at his side. Not unnaturally, in my opinion, I took this to be the Biblical character, Noah, leading his charges aboard the Ark two at a time. I was wrong. Tina happened to be writing a learned paper on another Biblical character at that time and informed me that my man was obviously Daniel and that the two animals were lions.

We left Shalfleet and went for a walk in the hills around Shorwell (which rhymes with coral) probably calling in the Crown Inn for a pint of beer as we usually do. One of these hills is called Mount Ararat and it was covered in a layer of greenery which Angela informed us was wild garlic. As she bent to pick up a handful to find which if any part of the plant had the familiar smell of garlic, a movement a few inches from her outstretched hand caught her eye and she saw it was a female adder. I was next to her and a whisper went down the line through Denise to Rob who, as always on walks, takes a large lead because of his long legs. The snake, as thick as my arm, reared its head, poised to strike and, for a few moments the only movement from any one us was Rob's unsuccessful attempt to take his camera from a back pocket in his jeans. The snake either thought better of attacking or decided that there was no need to and, as she retreated in coils back to the undergrowth, we all breathed again.

Despite being a highly qualified nurse, Angela suffers badly with bee stings and the like so, although the resultant poem was written with a large measure of attempted humour, it could easily have been a very serious incident - you find out who your friends are when you need some poison sucking out! Never mind, it gave us yet another Sicilian sonnet with *'The Angel and the Snake'*

The Angel and the Snake

Near Shorwell's Crown this Ararat was climbed
with thoughts of Noah's arch on Shalfleet's door
still dwelling, soon to be much later timed,
with Daniel and his lions to the fore.
Among the garlic leaves an Angel trod
then stooped, their wild aroma to inhale.
Alert, she saw the rising of a rod
once coiled and now erect, but not the male.
Those Hellish fangs and diamond back were clear
and, for a moment, terror struck her dumb.
Amidst all living things, when Death is near
an earthly Angel knows her time has come.
But, all the while, the snake was filled with fear
and turned to slip away. That is the sum.

Sometime in the mid 1970s I heard BBC Radio presenter, Johnny Walker, read an account of life as it was for the Native North Americans during the nineteenth century when all kinds of atrocities were inflicted upon them by European settlers. Since then I have had great respect for those people and this was enhanced a few years later when I heard a proverb which translates roughly as :-

'The mountains laugh when they see men fighting over who owns them'.

Eventually, these thoughts inspired a poem which, as is very frequently the case, was started then stalled after a stanza or two. In more recent times the matter of climate change has become more and more a news item with the current thinking of the so-called experts being that by some means the human population of this planet has been able to change the environment more dramatically in two centuries than it was able to do for itself in millions of years. As far as I can see, the internal combustion engine and the jet engine are the main scapegoats for an alleged act of murder when, as yet, no body has been found.

In trying to make some sense of all this, it occurred to me that my old North American friends may have unwittingly stumbled upon another truth. The proverb was obviously intended to refer to the take-over of land by one type of people from another, in that case Europeans from Native Americans. However, the same could clearly have been said of the eventual take-over by Homo Sapiens from Tyrannosaurus Rex and his subjects and I wonder if the same can also be said of the ultimate take-over bid – when, in the process of fighting each other, all the Nations of the World are united in defeating Earth itself.

Personally, I still have 'reservations' (sorry about the pun) about the consensus view of scientists as the recent changes may still yet prove to be cyclical as always before. However, if it is eventually shown to be true, and if our human activities really do end up having the potency to make a significant change to the planet, then it will be a Pyrrhic victory with the defeated mountains still laughing over the corpses of the men who achieved it.

Since I wrote *'Climate change'* I have come to know the poetic works of Felix Dennis with whom I seem to share a lot of views on the world and its people. I have a feeling he would agree with me on this one.

Climate change

I love to hear the mountains laugh
as men do battle at their feet.
What arrogance those microbes have
if they believe they own the peak.

For years unnumbered, hills have stood
and worn the clouds like coronets.
The flower of Man was not yet bud
when Earth gave forth those monoliths.

If permafrost becomes a bog
and mighty icebergs melt away,
can this be just because the fog
from Man's machines destroyed the sky?

For what is Man, how long has he
held court upon a global throne?
A day or less, compared to thee,
Oh Mother Nature, all alone.

Throughout your reign the ice has been
and gone again a hundred times.
Without the fossil fuels, my Queen,
would you stand guilty of these crimes?

And did the King of Lizards plot
to make his monarchy so brief
by living life the way he ought,
his only power those awesome teeth.

Should Daimler, Whittle and their kind,
accessories before the fact,
stand trial with Man, become enjoined
in charges made, their works knocked back?

We're as we are, we're of our age,
does not the Earth still spin and turn?
And so it shall on every page
of history, we shall come to learn.

Immediately prior to a holiday near Newquay in Cornwall with my friend Martin Round and his then wife, Susan, my then wife, Patricia, announced that she was expecting our first child. We had been married for over two years but for a long time before then I had carried the usual young man's fear of hearing those words! This was an entirely different matter and I was instantly filled with a sense of pride that has never left me since. A little out-pouring of emotion during the holiday worried me for an hour or two until Susan, a Registered Nurse, explained the effect of hormone changes on women. Or at least she explained to me that there were such things as hormone changes in women, I cannot claim to this day to understand them!

Right from the very start I was convinced that I was to have a son although we did discuss girls' names briefly. The baby was due in February and, as my paternal grandfather, Harold Claude, was born in that month I thought that Hayley Clare would give a daughter his initials as a tribute. For a boy, we liked the name Stephen but a cousin of mine with that name had died in an accident, aged 17, only a couple of years earlier and I thought that his brother or sister may wish to name their future offspring after him or, perhaps, 'retire' the name in his memory. Eventually my lad was named after the Duke of York who, as Prince Andrew, had also been born in the month of February.

'Fatherhood' was written in a site hut in Oswestry in the Autumn of 1979 and without any conscious awareness of the connections of that town to Wilfred Owen; he was born there in 1893. Ironically, I was there in connection with the demolition and partial redevelopment of a former army camp albeit one connected more with the Second World War than with the First.

The poem was revised slightly in late 1982 using a portable typewriter that I had recently bought and at that time I also wrote *'For Catherine'* with the intention of reading both at the joint baptism of my two children; not in church but at the party we held at home afterwards. However, a day of excessive celebration fuelled by gallons of my home-made wine, got in the way and both poems were consigned to the attic where they stayed until recently.

You may read later that my mother had a superstition based upon the proverb about counting chickens before they are hatched. I now hold to this very strongly myself and had clearly moved to that view by early 1982 as, although I knew that I must write a poem for my second child, as I had done for the first (a desire for equality or equivalence that I maintain to this day, even the poems, *'Fatherhood'* and *'For Catherine'* are both sonnets although the former is Sicilian and the latter is Shakespearean) I would not tempt fate by doing so before she had been safely delivered.

I do not recall where the name Catherine came from although she took her middle name, Ann, from her mother. However, I did expect her to become known as Kate. That happened at her own behest but only for about a fortnight circa 1992. She was born on a Sunday morning early in the Football Season and early enough in the day for me to play football or, more significantly, to announce to my team-mates the actual birthweight, upon which they had been running a sweep. She weighed in at 8lb 2oz and, fittingly, her Uncle Phil was the closest and took the kitty.

My parents were delighted with the boy/girl completeness of the family, with Mom actually pointing out that I had done exactly the same as Dad. I think I know what she meant! My sister, Lucy, already had the full set by then and the fact that her daughter, Donna, had arrived before her son, Paul, added to the symmetry and balance by virtue of the gender difference between Lucy and I. My dear mother had the ability to make everything in life seem rational and easily explained.

At the time of writing neither of my children has made so bold as to turn me into a grandfather although both have indicated an eventual intention to do so. If and when either or both do, I shall of course be delighted despite my falsely professed dislike of children between 5 and 15. It is only the badly-behaved ones in restaurants and public houses that I object to and I blame their parents anyway. My kids were great, they both knew how to behave in restaurants but unfortunately the only public houses we could take them to in those days were the ones which had what was laughingly called a family room. These were usually unheated and uncleaned out buildings!

I can only wish Andrew and Cathy and their respective partners the same symmetry and balance, and at least equal good fortune to that with which I have been blessed, in the quality and quantity of their own offspring.

Fatherhood

I can't believe that, after all these years,
I feel so proud that I shall be a dad.
His mom has sometimes shed some gentle tears.
"Just hormones," Sue says, "she is really glad"
I say 'his' with no doubt in me at all.
Some feeling deep inside me knows it's male
but, make no bones about this, I'd stand tall
to raise a little girl, her name I'd hail.
Stephen or Hayley, what shall be your name?
Her Majesty gave birth that time of year,
perhaps, for that, we'll call you just the same.
Andrew, you'd be, but you shall be no Peer.
So, son of mine, I shall teach you the game
and, when you're older, we shall share some beer.

For Catherine

I couldn't write this verse before you came.
I wish I had but never would tempt fate.
For sure, I would have loved you still the same
if you had been a boy and not my Kate.
My mom and dad produced the perfect set,
they shook my hand and kissed me for that match.
And Uncle Phil was pleased to win the bet,
on your birth weight, his winnings he would snatch!
It must be said, you are a lovely girl,
bonny and blithe and very full of grace,
perhaps, one day, your locks will show a curl.
If not, who cares? You are so fair of face.
And so my darling, Catherine, let me say
I'll be your rock forever, if I may.

I have mentioned 'Friends Reunited' earlier but that web-site has a spin-off which is now called 'Genes Reunited'.

Thanks to my father's cousin, Brian, I have a detailed and extensive record of that side of my family and I entered much of that information onto the web-site at an early stage. Brian had invested a great deal of time and money into researching the family history long before it became the fashion to do so and also long before it was made so much easier by the advent of computers and popularised by television programmes. Presumably because there are so many people listed on my tree, I regularly receive enquiries from people sharing names with members of my family and one such enquiry came in early 2005 from Jennifer Bullimore who wanted to know about Stanley Batty.

I explained that he had been married to a cousin of my father and that all I really knew about him, apart from the fact that he was a really nice chap, was that he used to live in Grantham and had two daughters, Tina and Gillian. Within minutes, Jen replied to my e mail message saying that she was in fact making the enquiry on behalf of the self-same Tina who was her life-long friend. Minutes later I received the first of what will eventually be a million messages from Tina herself. Her first thought was that I might be a previously unknown half-brother from a relationship that may have pre-dated the marriage of her parents: her mother was ten years her father's junior.

However, the picture very soon became clear. Tina and I just had to meet. She then lived in Grantham, where she had been born, but after university and marriage she had lived within 20 miles of me for over 30 years. I had known this and had intended for most of that time to present myself at her house on one of the countless occasions that I passed within yards of it. We arranged to meet somewhere between our current abodes, and a place just south of Derby, from where our common ancestors hailed, was chosen.

My father Dennis and his cousin Brian came along, together with all our respective partners. We spent an afternoon looking at old photographs and comparing almost forgotten memories. I was later able to establish that a lady called Dorothy who had contacted me to say that she thought her husband Desmond Woodall was descended from my great great great grandparents, Mathew and Susannah, was mistaken although I strongly suspect that there will prove to be a blood link a little further back.

We all resolved to meet at least annually and we bettered the first attendance figure in 2006 with my third cousin Beryl and her husband Peter joining us. Meeting her has opened up another rich vein of relatives, some in Australia, with whom I hope to become acquainted in due course. At subsequent meetings we have added Janet and her husband Colin, about whom there is more later, and Catherine and Vicky have also joined in.

Tina is actually is Christina Louise Negus (nee Batty) daughter of Margaret Batty (nee Woodall) and, like me, a great grandchild of Walter and Louisa (nee Slater) Woodall, a couple who feature in the poems that follow, along with several other family members including Tina's grandfather, Walter, and his younger brother Harold, who was my own grandfather.

Old Walter's mother was Christiana (nee Halliday) and whether intentionally or not, Tina therefore carries something very close to the names of two of our shared forebears. Old Walter died just before I was born and I understand that Tina's memory of him is very vague. My memory of Louisa is equally vague, as I was very young when we met in Derby on no more than half a dozen occasions. Tina, on the other hand, remembers her well but mainly as a kindly widow still wearing mourning clothes for Walter. She was a Derby girl and carried the accent to prove it.

I have many photographs of Louisa, one of which includes her son Harold, his son Dennis, and Dennis's son who is me. Another photograph includes Tina and Robert who were close contemporaries but a generation apart. Walter and Louisa had five children who survived to enjoy reasonably full lives and one, Evlyna, who died in childhood. Walter (the younger) married two ladies called Margaret and had a daughter, also called Margaret, by the first; she became Tina's mother.

Harold married May Leddington who gave birth to my father Dennis. Francis, always known by his middle name Leslie, married Hilda but had no issue. Alfred married Ethel (nee Stevenson) and had Brian and, eventually, Eva married William Birch and had Robert.

Despite being spectacularly attractive, or perhaps because of that, Eva's marriage came late in life and Robert was therefore only a few weeks older than Tina. Robert, who never married, died tragically at the age of thirty. He and I were born consecutively in the Woodall male line, separated only by Tina and her sister Gillian overall, but the ten year gap between us meant that I only knew him on roughly equal terms for a few years. It may have been in 1964 at the funeral of Alfred but it was more likely in 1966 at the funeral of Walter that my involvement with the Derby Woodalls as a near adult began.

By 1972 Robert was also dead but that gave me time to learn that he and I were not exactly soul-mates. On all of our encounters we had been friendly to each other but I always felt that there was a personality divergence between us that would prevent us becoming close friends even as the ten year age gap shrank to insignificance. It was chilling in 2005 to be shown a photograph of him taken circa 1949 in which he was wearing clothes that I had worn circa 1959 as his ever-thrifty mother handed them down to me as he grew out of them.

I was at his funeral and before we left Derby that day, Harold asked Dad and I to take him for a walk from Crewe Street, where Eva lived, to an area not far away called 'The Cavendish'. He stood and stared for a few minutes without speaking and then we left. When I arrived home from college the following evening I was met at the front door by Dad who told me that my dear 'Granddad' had died. He was 17 days short of his 77th birthday, had never fully retired and had cycled home to a cooked lunch, as he had done for more than 50 years, then died in his chair. Eva lasted another year and Leslie until 1975 when that generation came to a close.

However, I discovered, or at least thought I had discovered, that they had a cousin, Irene, who strongly features Eva at all earlier stages of life and who, at the time of my first meeting her, was a healthy 98 year old. There is more about Irene later but in brief, I can add that she turned out to be the daughter of a cousin rather than being, as I first thought, of the same generation as Harold. On my line we tend to breed in our late twenties whereas on the line that led to Irene it was usually in their early twenties. Over two of our generations, therefore, they managed to get three!

Anyway, I was inspired by the meeting to write a poem about it and I have given this the title **'Swarkstone'** which is where the meeting took place. It is certainly not a good poem but it did capture the day.

Swarkestone

Two leagues to the south of the Willn Street home
and five score years have passed.
The scions of Walter, Harold and Alfred are come
for each to meet each at last.

Only pictures from Leslie, for there was no son,
and Eva's did not endure
those decades whilst separate lives were run
and reunions were never sure.

The seed of Old Walter, with Louisa's blood,
flows through every vein
whilst they embrace, and talk, and choose the food
and drink that will them sustain.

Did Dennis know Tina when she was in youth,
or is it Margaret he means?
And of Ruffy the dog, oh, what is the truth?
Did she know him only from scenes?

Brian and Graham have been troubled by news,
from Dot who is married to Des,
that Mathew wed Mary when Susannah, we knew,
was his wife, the certificate says.

The afternoon flew, no-one noticed the rain,
and pictures were taken to keep
of the time that they met, and they will meet again
as love and blood both still run deep.

As a child I was enormously close to and very fond of my cousins. There were six of them, two of which I remember being born, with Robert being so named at my insistence. All came from my mother's siblings, Bert, Ernest and Norman as my father was an only child.

With my innate senses of equality and symmetry I always wished that I had Woodall cousins too and I have therefore been very happy to embrace Brian's children as such. Until Judith arrived in 1966 I had only Brian himself and another Robert, son of my Great Aunt Eva, to fill the gap and both were too much older than me to be truly regarded as equals within the family hierarchy. Stephen, the youngest of these cousins, was tragically killed in a car crash when he was seventeen and the oldest, Sylvia, died a couple of years later of a heart condition of which I had previously been oblivious.

Before then, at the age of thirty, my 'Woodall' Robert (whose surname was actually Birch) had been killed in a railway accident. The surviving Robert was always great fun and the source of a great deal of kindness to all family members. However, he succeeded in staying single until he was nearly fifty when he took us all by surprise by marrying. David and I were as close as brothers for thirty years until our marriages and the advent of our respective offspring progressively reduced the amount of time we had available to spend together. A little over a year older than me and always much larger, Dave was a massive influence on my development, a contribution for which I shall always be grateful. Patricia and Maureen were like sisters and deserve greater mention than I give them but I needed to save their names for the end, as you will see.

As Judith was joined by Victoria, Charlotte and eventually Matthew, a sense of family symmetry was beginning to emerge although it was to take several more years for them to reach ages at which the difference between us was immaterial. I am now close to and very fond of them all and with the added bonus of Tina coming into my life and with her sister Gillian at least in contact, it was time for a poem. The Latin title is, as you may by now guess, another tribute to Wilfred Owen but this one goes still further. It is a sort of double sonnet written in a form that very closely follows *'Dulce et Decorum Est'*. The last line is a conveniently appropriate version of 'Pro Patria Mori' using the names of my two surviving girl cousins on my mother's side. Corny? Contrived? Yes, guilty on both counts but who cares?

Consobrini mei

Numerically speaking, I had six
but two of Dad's produced the same again.
A dozen cousins is the current mix,
with more I hope to meet, I know not when.

Three girls like older sisters were to me
when we were young, but Sylvie grew not old
and Stephen, younger still, was first to see
the side of life that's better, so we're told.

Our Robert was for years a Peter Pan
who often speaks his mind but can be coy
and David and Goliath are one man,
a giant and my mentor. As a boy
he kept me free from harm and helped me plan
my life, my work and all that brought me joy.

Now I turn to those of paternal traits,
four known since they were born and two found late.
In truth our Gill is still unseen by me,
it will be sweet for us to meet one day.
But Tina shares my love of poetry
and is an artist too, with paint and clay.

The other four are closer on the map
(I speak of Charlotte, Vicky, Matt and Jude)
and younger but, with cousins, there's no gap
as ages are just numbers wrongly viewed.

So there you see them all, I've named the rest
of those that bring our forebears lasting glory.
But two more names I give with no less zest
Patricia and Maurie.

Fourteen months and eight days before I was born, my maternal grandmother had been blessed with her first grandson, three grand-daughters having arrived first. My cousin Dave was therefore part of my life from its very start and I was part of his from before his power of recollection commenced. We became inseparable friends and remained so through childhood and adolescence and well into our adult lives. We each played a role at the other's 1970s wedding and I am very happy that it was I who had first introduced him to his lovely wife, Glenda. Although many of the activities in which I had taken part throughout my life had been influenced by my slightly older cousin, including my choice of career, the fact that the first houses we owned after our respective marriages were virtually identical and within yards of each other was entirely fortuitous.

By the time we were about thirty, we had both moved to other parts and, more significantly, we had both started to raise a family. He started it with his son, Alex and he went on to produce Ben, but my son, Andrew, was only just behind so I have used a touch of licence in the poem that follows. I continued the sequence with a beautiful little daughter called Cathy and that point I retired from procreation whilst Dave went on to sire both Daniel and Ieuan. I have often marvelled at the way our combined offspring came to be born more or less in alphabetical order, with Ieuan covering several options in case I made a later comeback! The onset of such parental responsibilities left less and less time for socialising and the concomitant demands on our resources increased the necessity for us to use our shared education and training in the building industry to earn money and thereby maintain our respective broods at a decent standard of living.

But life moves on and the said offspring are now all adults, some even starting to nudge the age at which Dave and I started to lose touch. The reduction in day to day responsibility for them, coupled with the passing of our parents – his father being the only one of the four still alive – has had the compensatory effect of leaving us time to resume our brotherly friendship for the final phase of our lives. *'Blood Brothers'* sums it all up.

Blood Brothers

I had forgotten how it is
to have a friend so good.
Not just a friend, though that is fine,
but one who shares one's blood.
A friend who was a brother once,
until our fourth decade,
but then, for reasons never clear,
somehow became mislaid.

I think the pace of life itself
took us by sheer surprise.
We blinked and missed those many years
that sped before our eyes.
Producing children took our time
and there are six of those.
Five thorns, to use a metaphor,
around a lovely rose.

Five boys whose names fall into line,
two As, a B, then D,
before the lad with all the vowels.
One girl slots in at C.
Then there was work, with mouths to feed
and homes to build and keep.
We have to earn from what we learn
or watch our loved ones weep.

But children grow and leave the nest,
parents start to weaken
and dormant friendships shine again,
bright as any beacon.
The circle that is life itself
has almost turned around
but as we live the final arc
by blood we'll still be bound.

In 1975 the English political scene was grim to say the least. Not as grim as it was to become by 2007 but grim nonetheless. After what he always called 'thirteen years of Tory misrule' Harold Wilson just about managed to wrest power from a debilitated Conservative Party in 1964. Although returned as Prime Minister in 1974 after a four year interruption by Edward Heath, he was coming to the end of his period of power. The secret of his return to power was neither his ability nor his potential but the votes cast by a reluctant electorate which would clearly have preferred an old style, dependable Tory leader if there had been one around.

Heath never had the charisma and a significant number of voters were undoubtedly influenced by Johnny Speight's Alf Garnett referring to him as a 'Grammar School Twit'. Most of us Grammar School Twits preferred him to a politically misguided academic but there were too few of us to carry the vote, a situation partly created and certainly perpetuated by the cutting off of the supply of new 'twits' as Grammar School after Grammar School was closed.

But there were a few of us left and one of these had the advantage of being a girl. Margaret Thatcher successfully challenged for Heath's leadership of the Conservative Party and with Wilson gone and his avuncular but even more inept successor, James Callaghan unable to cling to power any longer, despite the help of the desperate-for-any-credibility Liberal Party, she became Prime Minister in 1979. Known as the 'Iron Lady', she did not suffer fools gladly and during her eleven years or so as Premier she succeeded in consigning the anachronistic trade union movement to a generation or more of emasculation. She introduced fairer income tax rates to encourage effort and initiative. She fought hard to make the rating system fair by introducing a charge equal for all persons although this was sabotaged by the Press which branded it 'a poll tax' (as if there would have been anything wrong with that) and she led the country to war with Argentina when its leader had the temerity to invade our outpost in the Falkland Islands as a diversion from his domestic crises. Margaret was born and raised in Grantham but for at least twenty years before I had even heard of her, 'Margaret of Grantham' was the name given to a cousin of my father to distinguish her from many other Margarets in the family. She was for us the personification of good taste and sophistication. The World was a better place when both ladies were in their prime. *'Gemini??'* (with double question marks to play down my twinning of these two disparate paragons) was written on a train from Lichfield to London, the journey and the composition taking precisely the same amount of time.

78

Gemini ??

The name of which I speak was known to all.
It was the cause of loathing, fear and scorn
but only from the scoundrels who did fall
beneath the iron hand, do not **them** mourn.
To others it meant help, relief, reward
and fairer tax on income and the poll.
Defeat to Galtieri and his horde
was handed out as wetter heads did roll.
By me the name was known before the rest.
It meant sophistication in all ways,
like eating eggs the way that is the best,
with cousins to be found in later days.
What **is** the name? It should be clear by now,
Margaret of Grantham: both are missed, and how!

My mother, Dorothy, was known by most as Dot although her brother, Ernest, always called her Doris. My little sister was baptised with the name Lynda but I have always called her Lucy so that must be a thing that big brothers do.

Mom was perpetually unfortunate. She was the fourth child and only daughter born in the depressed inter-war years in the same house as several other family members including me, some 23 years later, and Lucy three years after that - a day I remember very well. When Mom was ten years old her father was killed in an industrial accident which, these days, would probably make his widow a millionairess but which certainly did not at that time. Mom's three brothers were soon called away to war but by rare good fortune they all survived the hostilities. Her education was severely restricted by the family situation, by her gender and by the Luftwaffe which often caused loss of sleep during nights in a shelter which had to be made up during what should have been lesson time at school the next day. It was not restricted by her intellect. She had a good brain and an amazing ability to work out explanations for almost everything that life threw at her.

However, not all of her solutions were based upon fact as she was a lady of many superstitions. Her expression 'Don't have a black heart' still carries me through difficult times, meaning simply that to hold a grudge against someone achieves nothing more than to preserve and reiterate the offence that caused it. Against her wise counsel I once changed the date on my bedside calendar to show the correct date when I awoke the next morning. There could have been no other possible explanation for Karen Withers sinking her newly acquired and still sharp front teeth into my upper arm at school the next day. At no time in the half-century or so since, have I knowingly repeated the mistake. What is worse is that Karen evidently didn't care for the taste of my flesh because she never came that close to me again although she did marry a good friend of mine. I also recall many occasions when Dad was reprimanded for cutting his toe nails on a Sunday. I assume that the date changing superstition was based on the 'Counting chickens' proverb but I have absolutely no idea why nail-trimming on Sundays was bad luck. I once bought a red crash helmet with a white stripe in a jumble sale for five shillings but Mom made me add stripes of Dad's blue insulating tape before I wore it because red and white alone represented blood and bandages. Apparently a friend of Mom's sent her nephew, Duncan Edwards, some flowers in the red and white colours of Manchester United when he was in hospital after the Munich aeroplane crash of 1958. She blamed his death on the flowers and wanted to save me from the same fate.

Mom's answer to any question on history was 'Thomas á Becket' and her grasp of foreign languages more or less began and ended with an expression, 'Fermez la porte', used by an older work colleague at Messrs Adams and Benson Ltd where she was gainfully employed until her confinement with me. She suffered ill health for much of her life, especially after a seven month hospital stay in 1957/1958 as a result of the tuberculosis epidemic of that time. However, she was able to enjoy the relative comfort of her own house, a family car (although she never learned to drive) and holidays both abroad and in England during the second half of her life, including many in a 'continental frame tent' which was state of the art camping for the middle classes of the late 1960s and early 1970s. This was carried in a trailer towed behind Dad's Mark II Cortina over most of the South and South West of England during that period. Many of their visits to 'the Continent' were accompanied by her brother Ernest and his family. His first visits to that land mass had been made in uniform during the Second World War. He had seen active service throughout but, characteristically, rarely spoke about it.

In December 1990 I made a career change that raised my own standard of living considerably with immediate and long term effect but she died suddenly only six days later. Heavy snow had prevented me making a weekend visit and when Dad called to break the news to me in the early hours of a cold Monday morning there was still some road-clearing spadework to do before the funeral directors arrived to take charge. The only benefit she derived from my improved position was her one and only use of a cell phone. A mere fourteen years after we had first had a land-line telephone installed in the house she sat on the plush leather seats of my new car, a Ford Sapphire 2000E, and made a call to Lucy; I drove away with that image and never saw her alive again. She was a great admirer of Cousin Brian and the B.A. after his name. She was overwhelmed with pride when I achieved the same accolade. My B.A. is in Law and she was visibly disappointed when some years later I took the option of adopting the more explicit LL.B. instead. The subsequent academic achievements of her grand children would have been beyond her wildest dreams. Or would they? Another of her sayings was 'Always aim for the stars because you will always have the rooftops to land on if you miss' She was sixty one years and seven months old precisely when she died and I shall not knowingly change my calendar in advance until I at least match that age.

Hopefully the foregoing will help you make some sense of my poem, *'Dot'*.

Dot

Have not a blackened heart, my Son.
Change not the date till break of dawn.
No pedicure till Sabbath's done.
And red with white must not be worn.

Thomas á Becket was her key
to all that happened in the past.
'Fermez la porte' she said, with glee,
from Adams where her die was cast.

Such are the things my Mother said,
when I was young and keen to learn.
She also kept me clean and fed
my will to work and take my turn.

Then one cold night she left this life,
some thirty years too soon for me.
I lost the chance to ease the strife
that she'd endured continuously.

As if to lift my heavy load,
my fortunes rose, too late for Dot.
But all she said had made the road
for me to follow, from my cot.

As I approach her final age,
I wonder 'Shall I end the same?'
So words I set upon this page
act as letters after her name.

On September 12th 1953, Senator John Fitzgerald Kennedy married Jacqueline Bouvier in the United States of America. It was probably that event that prevented the World from reading that on the same day in Bartley Green, Denise Madeleine Cull was born. Family folklore has it that her forenames were those of her father's two favourite barmaids but Ernest Arthur Cull was also known to be a great admirer of the film star Madeline Carroll so, as far as I am concerned she was named after the actress, with the name 'Denise' being placed in front only because 'Madeleine' would have seemed pretentious in post-war working class Birmingham. They would not have been aware at that time that Miss Carroll was born only about five miles away in West Bromwich and that Madeleine was also her middle name, her first name being 'Edith'. With a French mother and a senior schoolmaster as a father, a posh name like 'Madeleine' would have been acceptable anyway.

In 1994, Denise became Mrs Woodall but had been a constant source of support and encouragement for my various endeavours for several years before then. Those endeavours of course include my work for the old school association of which preserving the memory of Madeleine Carroll was part, as I went to the same school as she did, albeit a couple of generations later. So, when I wrote **'Sonnet to an Old Throstle'** in honour of the older Madeleine, it became necessary for me to write one for the younger Madeleine too. Young Madeleine, or Denise if you insist, was known to her friends and family as 'Denny' until I inadvertently changed it to 'Deni' the first time I wrote it down. These days I usually call her 'Denzil' in private.

I am no Professor Higgins nor does she need one; she is an innately generous and caring person who gives freely of her time and money to those who need it but, like me, draws a line at scroungers and wastrels. This includes those who manipulate the 'nanny society' by taking out more than they need and certainly far more than they put in. She is in many ways like the mother-in-law that she hardly had time to get to know but whom she replaced in providing some measure of steadying influence on my reckless and outspoken ways. Unlike Dot, she was able to achieve the potential of her intellect by gaining a very good honours degree in Law despite a variety of domestic difficulties and concerns about her own health which are always present.

'The Class Act of '53', a Sicilian sonnet of course, is my small tribute to an amazing lady.

The Class Act of '53

There is a lady, as fair as any
that Pygmalion himself could create.
To most of us she is known as Deni -
wife, daughter, step-mum, sister, aunt or mate.
Kind of heart, she would give her last penny
to those who need help to postpone their fate.
Charity cases, although so many
deserve more funding to come from the State.
To give them aid of course she would borrow,
but not for those who would take it by stealth.
Her life has been touched by pain and sorrow,
bereavement, worry and fear for her health.
But through it all, she looks to tomorrow
and cares for others, their love is her wealth.

It should already be clear that, in my opinion, Wilfred Owen was one of the greatest poets that ever lived. I certainly regard two of his poems to be in the top three of the best poems ever written although I have changed my mind from time to time as to which one of the three is best. The trio is completed by a poem which must stand alongside Wordsworth's *'Daffodils'* as the one most frequently forced upon school children during much of the twentieth century. I refer of course to *'If'* by Rudyard Kipling. No prizes for guessing that the two from Owen are *'Anthem for Doomed Youth'* and one that I have already mentioned by way of an excuse for giving pretentious Latin titles to poems that will never be hailed as classics; I mean of course *'Dulce et Decorum Est'*. The line 'Across my world a shadow once was cast' came to me sometime in the middle to late 1960s, probably in 1968. It was inspired by a poem written by my close friend at the time, Lisbeth Brown, which was itself inspired by a film we saw together called *'On the Beach'* based upon a novel by Nevil Shute. Like most of our contemporaries, she and I, possibly out of conviction but more likely because it was fashionable, were strongly anti-war. Not being American and therefore having no direct right to speak about Vietnam, we focused our protests on the concept of a nuclear World War.

Lisbeth's poem started thus:-

The watery sun cast shadows on my bed
as I awoke, sat up, looked round and said
'I'm glad I'm alive'

It continued for several stanzas using the same last line and then with the final one ending 'I wish I were dead'. I once set this poem to music but by then the commercial appeal of protest songs had been exhausted by the likes of Dylan, Donovan, Baez, McGuire and even Buffy St.Marie so I didn't have to address the matter of shared royalties! I never did write the poem that I had intended to write but, instead, I eventually used the line to start one of my WW1 poems and, in deference to its age, I used part of it as the title of a book. The title of my poem in Latin is both another tribute to Owen and simply my way of saying that there is nothing 'great' about war. It translates simply as *'The Great War Was Not good'* You can easily work out the rest of it for yourself. Oh, and just for the record, it is yet another Shakespearean sonnet; you must by tired of them by now but I'm afraid there are still plenty to come.

Bellum Magnum Non Erat Bonum

Across my world a shadow once was cast
by The Great War, its name for twenty years.
As "Great" as Fire of London in the past
but worse than that, the cause of far more tears.
So why, when blades of mine were never honed
nor did I take the shrapnel and the gas,
am I compelled to speak in angry tones
of those four years that took so long to pass?
It's not because my brother fell in France
nor did my mother suffer widowhood.
And social change gave me a better chance
to rise than early bearers of my blood.
The reason for my wrath is simply said -
I mourn the countless rows of needless dead.

Also published in Ice Blue Mornings. Winter 2008

86

My various visits to Austria have already been mentioned, or at least some of them have - the skiing trips of my youth having been sidelined for now because of the paucity of poetry that came from them; there were a few but I can't remember them. During the same visit that spawned *'Salzkammergut'*, Denise and I took a bus to Bad Ischl one day, with mixed results. My grasp of the language proved to be insufficient to convince a pharmacist that there is in existence an effective remedy for heartburn without recourse to herbal preparations. On the positive side, we bumped into our friend, Rex Burton, with whom we shared coffee, cake and conversation for an hour or so. We also visited the Kaiservilla, the summer home of Emperor Franz Josef and his wife Elisabeth about whom more can be read later. Guided tours of the Kaiservilla were conducted regularly and the language used by the respective guides tended to be dictated by the nationality of the paying guests. It was clear that there was little demand for English and, although we are comfortable in German speaking restaurants and the like, a much wider vocabulary is needed for situations like that. We therefore took a guide sheet printed in English and did an unaccompanied tour between two German speaking parties. At one point, the party ahead had moved from the Emperor's study through one door at the precise moment that we had entered it through another. Unbelievably, we were alone in the room in which the declaration that acted as the whistle to start World War I was written. I could not resist breaking the house rules to sit in a leather chair that still bears the maccassa oil stains absorbed from the head of Franz Josef during his habitual afternoon naps.

The remainder of the tour of the house was perhaps less dramatic but certainly at least as revealing. I have no doubt that his pastimes were regarded as normal and acceptable at the time for a man of his rank, but this house proudly displayed the skulls of hundreds of chamois, numbered and dated, with the 2000th victim having been stuffed and mounted in whole! Franz Josef had come to the throne as a very young man and had soon gained a very beautiful and even younger wife. He was already an old man when he found himself in a position from which his only realistically possible course of action can now be seen to have led to the first major conflict of the twentieth century. His wife and son had both died in tragic circumstances, and when his nephew and heir, Franz Ferdinand, took the bullet of the Serbian, Gavrillo Princip, in Sarajevo, he must have felt that the end, which for him actually came two years later, had already arrived.

Back to Sicilian sonnet form then for ' *A Chair at Kaiservilla, Bad Ischl'*.

A Chair at Kaiservilla, Bad Ischl

I sat upon a peaceful leather chair.
For sixty years Franz Josef did the same
then rose, with war on Serbia to declare
but was it more than just another game?
He'd shot two thousand chamois, just for sport,
and countless other beasts and birds as well.
The Serbs had shot his nephew so he thought
that millions more should fall the way **he** fell.
He'd upset Russia when the chair was new
but had not made new Allies at that time.
His wife was dead and friends of his were few,
his own life was no longer at its prime.
Two years he saw, his heir another two
by when his world was mainly blood and lime.

There was a time when I thought that all the First World War poetry that was needed to be written had already been written and, more importantly, it had been written by participants in the conflict, though not necessarily active combatants. A.E.Housman, Rudyard Kipling, Jessie Pope and Vera Brittain are some of the names that spring to mind as non-fighters, for differing reasons but principally because they were too old or of the wrong gender.

(In the unlikely event that Shirley Williams ever reads this, I do hope that she will forgive me for including her brilliant mother's name in the same sentence as that of the rather silly Jessie Pope. There is no comparison between either the war effort or the literary skills of those two ladies.)

I later realised that millions of people, including me, know far more about that war than most of the poets associated with it could possibly have known. The incomparable Wilfred Owen, for example, never even knew the outcome of it nor any of its eventual consequences. He died in battle precisely one week before the Armistice and the church bells were ringing for victory and peace at the moment that his parents were given the news of his death. After this realisation I felt more comfortable and indeed more entitled to write on the subject but until then I had felt like an intruder: a cuckoo in the nest of a species that had been endangered for a century and which was now more or less extinct.

Nevertheless, the urge to write about 'The Great War' was irresistible and one of the products that emerged as a compromise was **'Pity'**.

Yet again, the title came from Owen as did the first line. It is in effect a summary of a dozen or so of the best known poems of World War I, written by some of the best known poets. Allusions to these men and to their work form the backbone of the poem but, I hope, I have given it a spin where necessary to underline my own views. I did originally write notes clarifying these allusions but I have decided not to include these here. Rather, I have taken the view that any reader sufficiently interested in the subject will either recognise them immediately or will derive some pleasure from having to think more deeply or even to indulge in a little research. To those, beware! There is one allusion to an earlier conflict as well as to writings that have nothing whatsoever to do with war but they do have relevance.

Pity

"All the poet can do is to warn"
said the boy from Salop, and he did.
Freed from Hell a week before the Dawn
of a world without war, they had said.
But a false dawn it was, not a doubt
had his friend with the Military Cross
who, in shock, had taught the boy to shout
of the madness, the killing, the loss.

A Cross for himself came to the boy,
for his bravery when back in the field,
made to sound more like a place of joy
than the bloodbath that flooded that weald
by one more doomed lad, who thought it grand,
and the doctor who died before Dawn.
It's poppies, they said, that grow in the land
that's part of England, but many still mourn.

The soldier who sniffed that saffron smoke,
and was felled by the famed guns of Loos,
knew that death was the end, the final stroke
given easy by those that can choose.
Mouthless, faceless, lifeless – blind to tears
are the dead and so shall they remain.
This boy saw much, in less than two years,
claiming inches of useless terrain.

A poor Jewish boy, and one weak in mind
were united in age and in thought
of the shame of a war of this awful kind,
men trenched with rats or on wire caught.
Those red wet things and verminous shirts
were visions that would trouble the sane.
So what fools were they who ordered such hurt?
Could they picture or suffer such pain?

Throughout it all, reading Latin and Greek,
the Professor at Cantab had stayed.
He lauded Ypres and shillings per week
but his lancer was differently paid.
A true Shropshire lad gave the bare facts,
a lie written in Latin exposed –
millions lost to meaningless pacts
whilst those men who had signed them reposed.

When introducing *'Summer of Love'* I referred to a second poem that had been inspired by a single incident occurring in 1967 and which lasted no more than five minutes from start to finish. The odd thing is that there was a gap of at least a decade between the final revision of the first poem and the germ of an idea for the second. From the date of the incident giving rise to the first poem, until the first publication of the second, the gap was just about four decades.

I refer of course to *'The Old Soldier'* which, I believe, needs little if any further introduction. It is certainly a sonnet, probably yet another Shakespearean sonnet, and has no hidden meanings whatsoever. However, it has a synergy with *'Summer of Love'*: a chance meeting of two people living geographically close to each other but having been born half a century apart.

To some extent, and certainly at different times, the fortunes of each were influenced by the other but not by equal amounts. At the time of the brief encounter it was taking me precisely forty eight minutes to earn two shillings as a part-time green grocer's assistant and the only things I had to spend it on were self-indulgent recreational items such as beer, cigarettes and gramophone records; I bought Beatles' singles as soon as they were released and Beatles' albums (LPs as we called them in those days) as soon as I could raise the money. I have no idea whether or not the other party spent a single day on the Somme, or four years entrenched there or nearby, or whether his injury and incapacity had come from an entirely different source. He may have been a total reprobate who got hurt performing some illicit act and whose obvious breathing difficulties stemmed from a lifetime of cigarette smoking.

My gift to him was very small indeed if his to me had been to endure a lifetime of suffering as a result of a genuine desire to give my generation a better life. However, if he had given himself a serious illness by a habit funded by, figuratively speaking, eventually getting his hand caught in the till, then I was the more generous. I know which version I prefer to believe and for it I thank you, Old Soldier!

The Old Soldier

"You're in the Staffords now," the Sergeant said,
a shilling placed within the young man's hands.
And **too** young, by the way, but he'd been led
to list for King and Country by the band.
At eighteen almost all of him came back
with liquid lungs and half an arm blown off
by German lads with orders to attack.
His sweetheart couldn't bear to hear his cough.
For fifty years, he's trudged the park alone
as work and love have rarely passed his way.
Although the sunshine warms his aching bones
the sadness in his heart won't go away.
A kind young man puts two bob in his hand:
perhaps it **was** worthwhile to make that stand.

I think that I have always known the name 'Victor Silvester'. He was a dance band leader serving a generation before my own interests in such mating rituals commenced. By my time, the beat was being provided by the likes of Chris Farlowe and the Thunderbirds at the West Bromwich Adelphi, embryonic stars such as the Move and the Moody Blues at the Handsworth Plaza and icons like the Beatles at Birmingham Odeon which, in December 1965, were the headline act of the first ever pop concert that I attended. Both dancing, even in the aisles, and listening to the music were prevented by the hysterical behaviour of hundreds of adolescent girls, screaming like the Sabine women should have screamed, whilst pledging themselves to one or all of the Fab Four.

Dances like the Twist and the Shake did not rely upon the roll-out mat showing foot positions that the Quickstep and the Foxtrot required. To the indignation of my dad, one of my girlfriends once referred to those as 'Old Time Dances', a genre which for him meant those dances that included the Polka and the Gay Gordons. I cannot recall how it came about, nor when, but many years after I had last heard his name mentioned in any context, I learned that Victor Silvester, who was named in celebration of the victorious outcome of the Boer War so I am given to understand, was a boy soldier in World War I and before he was actually old enough to enrol, other than by lying about his age, he had been put on several firing squads to dispatch fellow soldiers accused of cowardice in the field.

In his autobiography, entitled *'Dancing is my life'*, he recalls a particular execution, the first in which he participated, in some detail and this is the basis of my poem.

In my research I of course learned that his story has been challenged for its truth and that some have put forward convincing cases to the effect that his army career lasted only as long as it took his mother to track him down and bring him home. I did write a sixth verse to *'Silvester'* which started with the line:-

'Lies, lies, nowt but lies'

but I scrapped it within days of writing – I never could see a good reason to allow facts to get in the way of a good story!

Silvester

"Left…. Left….. Left, Right, Left"
the subaltern barked as the squad marched out.
The dawn sun shone through a cleft
in the cloud that shrouded this latest bout
of death dealt by those bereft
of care, compassion, common sense or doubt.

Guns were raised, orders given,
trigger fingers twitched on trembling hands.
Shots rang out, loud and even,
to send a scared boy to the promised land.
Alive, praying for heaven,
the boy dragged his chair across wet, red sand.

But the subaltern caught him
in two quick strides. Then one close range bullet
and the weak dawn light grew dim.
Now with blood or tears all eyes were full, it
made them weak in heart and limb
and their breakfast to rise in the gullet.

One squad lad had served three years
but he was just seventeen at the time.
Four times more he, with his peers,
had to play in this evil pantomime.
Sent home hurt, Mum in tears,
playing truant to sign up was **his** crime.

"Slow….Slow…. Quick, Quick, Slow"
His new dancing beat was known to them all
in the Palais de Danse so
the Theatre of War turned into a ball.
Light of foot, he beat the foe
and his name is not on Thiepval's wall

There are many songs that I wish I had written, lyrics, music or both. Most genres are covered by that wish – Classics, Operatic, Rock, Popular and Folk to name but a few.

There are many goals that I wish I had scored, David Beckham's for England against Greece in 2001 probably heading that particularly long list, with Jeff Astle's against Everton at Wembley in the 1968 F.A. Cup Final running it a close second. David Platt's against Belgium in the 1990 World Cup is also in the running. The set of six scored by George Best against Northampton in a cup game immediately upon his return from a 28 day suspension was to die for and I always find it amusing, when I see the recording of that game, that my friend and former WBA defender, Ray Fairfax, who was marking George that day, can be seen in the frame for only one of those goals and then for less than 1 second! Many years later, the Sunday newspapers carried a picture of Michael Owen about to score his fourth for Liverpool in a 6 nil thrashing of the Baggies. Many individuals in the crowd including my son Andrew, who was coached in his younger days by Ray Fairfax, could be seen in the picture but not a single Baggies' defender!

There are many people from all eras that I wish I had met – Jesus of Nazareth, Saint Ralph Sherwin, Isaac Newton, Isambard Kingdom Brunel, Prince Albert, Winston Churchill, Madeleine Carroll, John Lennon and Margaret Thatcher for examples, and each for entirely different reasons.

Needless to say, there are also many poems that I wish I had written, most of these having been referred to elsewhere in this book. However, there is one in particular that, in this category, stands above all others and I have neither referred nor alluded to it earlier but I include it here in full for you, dear reader, to savour and I have no doubt to admire as much as I do. Its author is none other than my darling wife Denise whose talents have never ceased to astonish me. I am so full of admiration for her as a professional and as an academic that I am sometimes guilty of overlooking the fact that she is a wonderful wife and one hell of a sexy lady!

But I digress. *'I can't stop thinking'* is all hers. It needs no explanation nor any further introduction. Privately, I love the concept of an intelligent twenty first century woman putting Jessie Pope and her ilk in their place. White feathers indeed! What say you to that, my lady? This poem is brilliant, evocative, simple but all-embracing and, above all, it could only have been written by one person, my Deni.

I can't stop thinking………

I can't stop thinking about the men in the trenches,
the lice, the vermin, the barbed wire fences.
They should be home canoodling with wenches.
I can't stop thinking about the men in the trenches

I can't stop thinking about the boys on The Somme,
Ypres or Mons, they all merge into one.
Millions of mothers losing their son.
I can't stop thinking about the boys on The Somme.

I can't stop thinking about the sweethearts and wives
left at home, as they were, to get on with their lives.
The horror of war their future deprives.
I can't stop thinking about the sweethearts and wives

I can't stop thinking about those who were shot.
Not by the enemy but by those who had not
the compassion to recognise these poor wretches' lot
I can't stop thinking about those who were shot.

I can't stop thinking that war is not right.
Far better to talk than to take up the fight.
Ignore the misguided with their feathers of white.
I can't stop thinking that war is not right.

I can't stop thinking………

by Denise M. Woodall

Writing poetry can be addictive. Felix Dennis only came to it at the age of fifty one and now claims to spend an average of four hours every day writing it. Certainly his prolific outpouring of very good quality poems bears testimony to the truth of that claim. By my own estimate he must be approaching two thousand poems up to now and, having read more than half of them, I can say for sure that the standard remains consistently high and, above all, they retain structure without resorting to the pretentious blurb that many other famous and contemporary poets trot out and, also, without any one of his poems sounding as if it had been lifted from a cheap greetings card. He is justifiably proud of those facts as he will surely tell you if you ever have the great pleasure of going to one of his readings.

Denise was slightly older than Felix when she wrote *'I can't stop thinking'* but, like him, she was recovering from a serious illness at the time. Another thing they have in common is an apparent predilection to addiction as she too found that she couldn't stop at the one. At that point the similarities end except for the shared ability to maintain a high standard of writing. The difference is one of scale as, some four years after Denise's first, her waiting readership was treated to her second. On that basis we could extrapolate her output to four poems over twelve years, which is quite a few short of Felix's total over the same period, but we must also bear in mind that she doesn't spend four hours a day writing. Instead, she waits for the muse to descend and then completes the work in a matter of minutes.

So it was with *'To Leah Louisa'*. At about 4.00 a.m. one morning I was eased from a shallow sleep by Denise enquiring as to whether or not I was awake; I am sure most readers will have had a similar experience with their own partners for one reason or another. Her reason on this occasion was to tell me that a poem had come to her and, obviously, I did the only thing I could in those circumstances and reached for the notebook and pen that I always keep by my bed on the off chance that the same thing might happen to me.

Leah Louisa was Denise's grandmother on her father's side who died about forty five years ago but of whom Denise was very fond. Denise's father, Ernie, was a son of her second marriage, she having become a widow of the Great War in 1915. She became a widow again in 1940 and this was in all probability to be blamed on the same war as her second husband, Ernest Edward, had been gassed in the trenches and died of lung problems at an early age. A few years ago Denise and I located their shared grave and have been the only visitors to it two or three times a year since, with each visit making Denise fonder of her 'Nanny Cull'. That is what the poem is all about.

To Leah Louisa

So few moments to recall
Even fewer pictures to remind
Only a gravestone to visit
No film to rewind

And yet a bond grows between us
As the puzzle is pieced together
Not just a proud admiration
But a love that will last forever

by Denise M. Woodall

As I did with **'Pity'**, I wrote explanatory notes for **'Isandlwana'** but I have not reproduced them here in full. I first saw the film **'Zulu'** soon after it was released in 1964 and I would estimate that I have watched it on average once every three years since then, including once with sub-titles one rainy day on holiday somewhere in mainland Europe.

'Isandlwana' actually has more in common with the later and less well known film, **'Zulu Dawn'**, to the extent that it only mentions the Rorke's Drift affair in passing. Whilst this remarkable event, comparable in many ways to the Dunkirk retreat sixty years later, was both commendable and indeed well commended, it was a useful tool with which those responsible for the embarrassing reversals elsewhere could deflect censure. Sir Bartle Frere and Lord Chelmsford were the two principals in the pantomime that was the battle of Isandlwana. Although Frere's guilt is the greater for the simple reason that his actions were the main cause of the Zulu wars, Chelmsford's inept handling of his forces in the field, the effect in no way mitigated by the actions of some of his lieutenants, was the more proximate cause of heavy losses.

I met Professor Sheppard Frere, a descendant of Sir Bartle Frere, in 2007, not, as you may think, in connection with Andrew's degrees in archaeology and Roman History in which Professor Frere is a leading expert, but because his Insurers sent me along to his house in Oxford to advise on the flood damage he had suffered that summer. As I looked at the various awards that had been made to his great grandfather sitting on his sideboard I felt slightly guilty at the words I had written a few years earlier. After some thought I decided it would be best not to send him a copy of **'Isandlwana'**. He was over ninety years old at the time and he told me that, although he expected to reach ninety five, he didn't expect to emulate his mother and pass the century mark. He is as friendly as he is accomplished and I hope he is wrong.

It is very sad to reflect that few lessons had been learned by the British Army thirty five years after the Zulu affair when it was faced in the field of conflict by a much more equally armed opponent. It is one of life's ironies that almost all of the leading players in this particular Act from the full British War Drama died either young, disgraced or both. The exception was Lord Chelmsford who lived long enough to see the Boer War and the accession to the throne of Edward VII before dying at a ripe old age whilst playing billiards in his London club. As a poem, **'Isandlwana'** needs several out loud readings for familiarisation but after that I hope you like the form and rhythm of it.

Isandlwana

Bring Boer, Black and British folk under one rule
was the task set for Sir Bartle Frere.
Forty thousand Zulus, an army in fact,
did not wish to yield nor to sign such a pact.
"Without a war" had said London, worried elsewhere,
but the Consul knew no other tool.

Cetshwayo was told to disband or else
the might of the Empire he would feel.
No concession like that could be made, Bartle knew,
as the British were trained but relatively few.
So Lord Chelmsford, who before his Empress would kneel,
invaded, as Trollope later tells.

At one mile per day they reached Isandlwana Hill
and established base camp for the fray.
Two thirds of the force was sent off south east
but north east and close were twenty thousand at least.
They were spotted by scouts so attacked the same day.
The camp fought back but chances were nil.

Warnings went out but by Chelmsford dismissed
then news of the attack was relayed
to Colonel Harness who sent a relief squad back
but was stopped by the Peer who denied the attack.
At the camp, fierce fighting meant the full price was paid
by hundreds of men, now on a list.

Izimpondo zankomo is how they describe
the shape of the attack by the horde.
The horns of the buffalo contain the defence
whilst pressure is applied by the head, much more dense.
With twelve men to one into the base camp they poured,
spears won the day - but guns halved the tribe.

A gross of good soldiers was grudgingly led
to defend Rorke's Drift from attack.
Chard and Bromhead were equals in both station and rank
but the lower class Dalton is whom they must thank.
He inspired the men to force the horde back
again and again, as the soil turned red.

Not a victory as such, just a solid defence
but to Chelmsford it provided support.
In his swift note to London he reported this ace,
over King Cetshwayo, to avoid the disgrace.
Chard and Bromhead's loyal silence with medals was bought;
Dalton's VC was to stay future tense.

Politicians and press were united at home
in demands for Lord Chelmsford's recall.
Lord Beaconsfield was alone in resisting this cry,
to avoid the Queen's wrath he joined in with the lie.
Dead Durnford was damned for Isandlwana's fall;
and shortage of shot for the tombs.

Weakened by illness and by political swing
the Prime Minister altered his stance.
Chelmsford was replaced under African skies
then to Victoria at home he dealt a pack of lies.
She showered him with honours as if in his trance,
he was her hero and under her wing.

With Gladstone back in power and Beaconsfield dead,
Consul Frere was sacked and disgraced.
Cetshwayo was exiled, and Dalton died sad,
and the real Rorke's Drift heroes were only a fad.
Chelmsford lived longer but then died in a haste
at his club, with a cannon off red.

For any reader who has remained to this stage of the book I have got some great news – it is almost half-time!

You will by now have formed some opinion of me and you will have identified some of my main interests in life. You will have found that although I have regarded Lichfield as my home for many years, I was born and raised in West Bromwich and that I still have very close ties with both its leading school and its football club.

It will not have escaped your notice that I have travelled a good deal but that I have never been massively impressed with other parts of the World. In the second half you will see that there is an exception to this. It is also self-evident that I managed to avoid being brain-washed by the so-called comics of the 1950s in each of which some gung-ho sergeant or wing commander murdered a few dozen of their German or Japanese counterparts in every issue. Even as a child I was never comfortable with that type of jingoism and by the mid 1960s I had become very strongly anti-war. Fortunately, it was fashionable to think that way at the time but I was naturally very comfortable with the 'Make love not war' ideal, on both counts. Nevertheless I loved Johnny Speight's line about us beating the Germans in two World Wars and one World Cup; a sense of humour is essential. Sadly, there never has been anything remotely amusing about the Japanese.

'An die Gefallenen' grew out of two events within six months of each other and brings together several of the interests mentioned above. In November 2005, the beautiful oak-clad pipe organ in my old school hall which had been built in remembrance of former pupils who died in World War I, and which had panels added later to include victims of World War II, was officially registered as a War Memorial and a service of re-dedication was held. I had walked, pedalled or driven my Vespa the mile from my family home to the school many times during my years as a pupil there and it was a privilege to make the slightly longer journey that day. In May 2006 I found myself in Saint Wolfgang's Church in Salzkammergut looking at another organ, this one being beautiful in its own way but surprising metallic in appearance. Close to it were the lists of local lads who died in the World Wars and two facts hit me right between the eyes. Perhaps obviously, boys of the same tender ages as our own fallen were mourned by our erstwhile enemy and, more significantly, the sons of some of the ones on the first list appeared on the second. When will we ever learn? This is one of my favourite poems, written in English but with a German title, to the fallen.

An die Gefallenen

I know two organs, far apart
in distance and in style.
One by a lake in Osterreich
and one, from home, a mile.

The nearer one is cloaked with oak
the other gilded bright.
With finials and angels fair
to match that splendid site.

Two organs, so, two towns of course,
each one is home for some.
And both were home to others once,
before their time had come.

The wood belonged beside the lake,
the metal near the foundry.
Yet each town used the other's craft,
it seems taste knows no boundary.

Each organ has two lists nearby,
the names of those who fell.
Auer und Weis, Adams and Wood;
for those there was no bell.

The later lists are larger yet,
as lessons were not learned.
Auer and Wood are there again,
their fathers' murders spurned.

I must have been vaguely aware of the existence of Emperor Franz- Josef from the first time that I heard about the causes of the Great War. However, the first time that I recall having consciously registered him was in 1975 on a skiing trip to the small village of Nauders, near to Switzerland's St. Moritz but actually in Austria, and also very close to the Italian border. In those pre-Euro days, his face seemed to be on every banknote, every postage stamp and on one in every five street names. Considering the fact that he had been dead for nearly sixty years by then, it seemed to me to be a remarkable memorial matched only, in that part of the World, by Mozart himself.

However, he had been over-shadowed in my mind by another Emperor, Kaiser Wilhelm II, to the extent that I had almost forgotten that the delightful Austrians had not only been batting for the other side in the Great War but that they had actually started it! The intervention of World War II and the embarrassment of sharing a Nationality with Herr Hitler probably served to make the people I would meet deceptively pro-English. I have often thought how clever it has been of them to convince the World that the German Mozart was Austrian whereas the Austrian Hitler was German!

Poor old Franz-Josef had also been over-shadowed by his nephew and heir, Franz-Ferdinand, whose only contribution to history, apart from throwing a tantrum over whom he should marry, was to take Princip's bullet in Sarajevo. At least one historian of my past acquaintance attributes even that to a faulty gearbox on his Renault which prevented his driver engaging reverse gear at a time when retreat would have been a great move.

Nevertheless, Franz-Josef ruled his Empire for even longer than Queen Victoria ruled Britannia, and made relatively few mistakes. One of these was in falling out with the Russians early in his reign. This was not a bad move in itself but made much worse, eventually terminal, by failing to replace them as friends with any significantly powerful race. It did not occur to me for some considerable time that this guy was a serial runner-up and that he had already been upstaged.

First by his loopy son who had entered a suicide pact with a very young girlfriend at their 'holiday home', Mayerling.

Second, and this is where I come to the point, also by his beautiful, intelligent and accomplished wife, Elisabeth.

Elisabeth of Bavaria was, relatively speaking, of lesser aristocracy than Franz-Josef although they were cousins. She was a World-class horsewoman whilst his sporting trophies comprise nothing more than the stuffed or otherwise preserved remains of thousands of helpless creatures. I am not talking about the victims of his war here, just the birds and animals he proudly shot, like fish in a barrel, on his estates. The similarities between Elisabeth, who was usually known as Sisi, and Diana, Princess of Wales are astonishing: in some ways not unlike those famous ones between Abraham Lincoln and John Kennedy. Beautiful, dutiful and dynastically directed, maritally unhappy, narcissistically frustrated by age and gravity and, ultimately, the victim of a violent end shrouded with intrigue and perpetuated by conspiracy theories. Sisi was evidently the more intelligent of these two unfortunate ladies and spent many of her lonely hours writing poetry in preference to whinging to any nineteenth century equivalent of Andrew Morton or Martin Bashir, although it seems that she did her fair share of cosying up to the Will Carlings and James Hewitts of the day! For example, there was 'Bay' Middleton who was later suggested by many as being the real father of Winston Churchill's wife, Clementine Hosier.

I have taken some of these poems and their literal translations into English and re-written them. It is quite beyond my linguistic abilities to make a serious attempt at true translations that would also retain the poetic form of the original German. I have therefore concentrated on the poetry rather than the grammar in most cases.

My own resultant English versions have the same metres and rhyming patterns as Sisi's originals had, as far as reasonably possible, but I have also attempted in places to both broaden and to modernise her work. The titles are nearly all my own inventions although *'Titania's Spinning Song'* owes more to Shakespeare than to either Sisi or me.

From the selection of short poems that follow, the sadness of this bird in a gilded cage can be sensed. Collectively, I call them *'The Sisi Set'.*

Imagine her with fading, film-star looks sitting alone in some of the most beautiful palaces and gardens on Earth, owned by her husband as the long-established head of one of the most powerful empires on Earth but for whom she appears to have had little affection. It does have a familiar ring to it, I think.

106

Longing

Fresh Spring returns, splendid beyond words,
which trims the trees with new green hue
and teaches new songs to this year's birds
and makes the flowers glow with dew

But what can Springtime bliss be to me
here in this distant land so strange?
I long for the Sun of home, you see,
I long for that river's soft range.

The Path

Oh had I but never left the path
that would have led me to be free
Oh that on the broad way of this wrath
and pride I never came to be.

I have awakened in a prison
with golden chains which bind, I see.
But now my yearning always is on
freedom which turned away from me

I have awakened from a rapture
which did my youthful spirit stay.
And, vainly, do I curse that capture
in which I bet freedom away

Abandoned

In my great loneliness I dwell
and I make my songs alone
My heart with grief and sadness fills
and weighs my spirit down

Once I was so young and richly
blessed with love of life and hope.
Nothing matched my strength and keenly
with the open world I coped

I loved, I lived, and loved some more
as through the World I wandered
But never reached what I strove for
as truths were ever squandered.

Peace

Sweden, Oh life is better there,
we shall always envy you.
Across the sea without a care
the good folk are happy too.

Their rulers can admit with pride
that many lives have been saved.
True, armies do not there abide
and cannon strength has been waived.

Only in Bulgaria?

The poorest farm folk sweat,
working their fields of soil
in vain, for they never get
returns for all their toil.

Bullets, guns and bombs cost dear
with thousands used each day.
Especially with voting near,
to win the game their way.

Who knows, without our leaders
would there still be battles?
For costly war no need as
Victory's urge is settled.

Love and Wine

For me there is no love
nor wine for laughter.
They either give me pain
or sickness after.

Love can be sweet, but sour
and bitter it grows.
My wine is doctored but
helps me keep those vows.

Falser still than wine
often can be love.
We may pretend to kiss
but as thieves we move.

For me there is no love
nor wine for laughter.
They either give me pain
or sickness after

Love, lust or lucre?

As I do not believe in love,
what makes your life so sour
are different urges that will prove
to be your lack of power.

My boy, you surely are in debt
as you imagine, slyly,
that I, your Queen, will always let
your charms be valued highly.

Titania's Spinning Song

You want a game of love,
misguided man with feet of clay?
With golden threads I wove
your death-cloak, yesterday.

Within my pretty trap,
enmesh yourself then die
while I stand by and clap
from dawn till dusk, but cry.

To my husband

Oh, man of mine, please let me know
what could make you inspired?
It seems to me, but is it so,
your pulling power is tired?

The sickly ass you set to pull
cannot take you much further
you're fast in mud, up to your hull,
oh would it not be smarter
for you to catch the noble steed
here on the open meadow
and force the bit between her teeth
today and not tomorrow?

As, once before, she beat the soil
and freed your carriage for you.
So chase away that short, fat mule
that sticks to fools like horse glue.

I see you

I see you riding, sad and serious
on this winter night in deepest snow.
The wind is blowing, fast and furious,
my heart is aching and full of woe.

In the dark East, pallid-lurid and blurred
another pale day is now dawning.
Your leaden heart, made heavy by your words
goes home to hear a bitter warning.

That night – long, long ago

Do you remember that night at the dance
where, all at once, your soul met mine by chance?
Long, long ago. Long ago.

Where our strange and distant friendship began;
do you, my friend, think of it when you can?
Long, long ago. Long ago

Think you of words so deep, so intimate
that we exchanged as music played till late?
Long, long ago. Long ago.

Once more we pressed hands but I had to fly,
nor could I show my face, I don't know why.
Long, long ago. Long ago

Instead I lighted up my very soul;
Friend, that was more, more than my mortal whole.
Long, long ago. Long ago.

Years passed and disappeared, as they do,
but not again did they unite us two.
Long, long ago. Long ago.

Searching at night, my gaze questioned the stars
but no news came from them, Venus or Mars.
Long, long ago. Long ago.

Sometimes I thought you near, and sometimes far,
dwelt you, perhaps, beyond another star.
Long, long ago. Long ago.

If you still live, give me sign by day
that I can hardly hope for or expect.
Friend, come to me once more and show respect.

Having enjoyed a holiday in Vienna in 2006 we decided to explore Prague a year later. Denise and I tended to take Autumn holidays with my cousin Maureen and her husband, Steve. Maureen was a teacher and, as such, found it hard to take holidays or days off when her school was open for business. Our Autumn holiday therefore tended to be during half-term and in this respect differed from all our other holidays which are planned to coincide with school-time in order that we can avoid most under sixteens and save a few pounds at the same time.

But I digress; a few days before we left for Prague it was becoming clear that my father's illness was serious. He had complained of hip pains and constipation for weeks and had briefly referred to what he insisted was a 'slight anomaly' in his right lung. He spent about fifty years prior to 1990 smoking cigarettes, something of a family tradition as his father and uncles could have smoked for Great Britain if it had ever been made an Olympic event, and my obvious and immediate concern was that lung cancer had finally kicked in.

Despite some resistance, I resolved that I would be present myself at all future meetings with Dad's medical advisers, to ensure that the right questions were asked and that full answers were given. However, the next appointment was already set to take place on my second day in Prague so my sister went along instead. At this point it might be useful to mention once again that my sister's name is Lynda but that she calls herself Lynn and I call her Lucy. She discussed Dad's case with his doctor and was left in no doubt but that he did indeed have lung cancer and although she didn't intend to tell me the facts until I had returned from holiday, she would never lie to me and therefore gave me the facts in response to my text message of enquiry whilst the four of us were walking through the old town of Prague.

The exchange of messages started as we walked by the Powder Tower and was complete by the time we reached the river. It was not just the weird architecture that had impressed me by that time, exaggerated Gothic like the castles seen in cartoon films, but also the people. The ladies were of uncommon beauty, all very tall with pretty faces framed by long blonde hair and the men were smartly turned out and well groomed. Jeuri, our guide on a sight-seeing trip around the city, explained that the World's impression of Prague and its people was inaccurate and had only been created by, and for the duration of, the short period of history during which it was under the control of the Soviet Union. Prague is and always had been a West-European city.

118

Jeuri also mentioned that the Roman Catholic Church was actively searching for evidence that the former pope, John Paul II, had been responsible for at least two miracles as that would qualify him for canonisation in considerably less time than it usually takes. As you will read later, it can take centuries!

I think that Richard Dawkins would describe me as a pantheist but, if not that, then monotheism has an attraction provided that we keep well clear of the image of a chap with a long white beard sitting on a cloud. Therein lies the problem I have with both Roman Catholicism and the Protestant High Church, between which I could never see enough difference to justify all the blood that has been spilled arguing over minor details.

In short, what I mean is that if you believe in a personal god then leave it at that and do not complicate the situation by promoting mere mortals to some elevated position, above the rest of us but below God, either as saints after they are dead and gone or as popes whilst they are still alive. In my view miracles do not happen but if you believe that they do then give God the credit and do not contrive to attribute something or another to a very nice ex-goalkeeper from Poland.

You will appreciate from the foregoing words that my religious beliefs are not entirely orthodox although I was comfortable with the Primitive Methodism that I knew in my younger days and which still endures in a few kind hearts today. Such was my despair at the news about my father that when we reached the plaque on the Charles Bridge parapet that, according to legend, has the power to grant wishes made whilst rubbing it with the hand, I went for it and asked in all seriousness and sincerity that it would transpire that the doctors were wrong. I swore at the same time that if my wish should be granted then I would write an affidavit or whatever oath might be considered appropriate to the Vatican, giving credit to John Paul II for what would have been his greatest ever save.

Many years earlier, on a wet Wednesday afternoon in Rome, Denise had taken my photograph in front of Saint Peter's Basilica. Over my left shoulder a tiny figure dressed in white can be seen in the distance and I have always referred to this as my having had my photograph taken with the Pope in much the same way as I treasure the video footage of David Beckham and I at Old Trafford although he was taking a corner and I was sitting in the fourth row of the stand watching him.

A band was playing on the bridge as we walked across and this prompted me to join in a Charleston with Denise, much to the amusement of our fellow tourists. I think I may have been slightly hysterical, if a man can ever be hysterical, at the time as dancing is not an activity that I do much of, even in more conventional circumstances.

Over the next few days we saw the rest of that fine city, including the Astronomical Clock which chimes, apparently randomly, any number of times. From the tower above it I was struck by the similarly of the city roof scene to that which can be seen from the Camponile in Florence except for the rough, dark chimneys. Steve has a dodgy back and Maureen and I have very suspect knees so we took the lifts in two stages to the top, the upper lift having glass walls. In the poem which follows, I refer to an elevator in the hope that my compatriots will understand that my American readers do struggle with certain simple words. Anyway, 'elevator' has the right number of syllables!

I walked down alone so that I could inspect the strengthening work that had been done to the old structure, including an internal steel-reinforced concrete frame and the lift-shaft formed by six steel spirals, like three double helices. As is now possible in most parts of the World, or at least in those parts that I am likely to visit, we had a decent lunch one day, a chip butty and a pint of Guinness to be precise, and a ride in an open horse-drawn carriage, the hairless heads of Steve and I being protected against the bitter cold by hats from the C and A store near our hotel on Wenceslas Square.

By chance, or maybe they do it all the time to keep the tourists happy, there was performance of the 9th Symphony by local lad, Antonin Dvorak, being staged while we were in Prague, so we took the opportunity of getting tickets to attend. Brown bread will never taste the same again!

Obviously a poem emerged soon after I came home and, with a nod of thanks to the late Freddie Mercury, and also, I suppose, to Homer, for the title.

'Bohemian Odyssey' tells the story...................

Bohemian Odyssey

Prague's girls are long in leg and fair of face
and elegantly dressed, despite the cold.
The menfolk, too, describe their Russian style
as myth – they are now Western, as of old.
Its concrete structures stand like Eastern blocks
outside the Gothic town of fairy tales –
from Powder Tower down to Charles's bridge,
a walk I make as Father's fitness fails,
the pinkness of the stone by smoke made black
like smokers' lungs from countless cigarettes.
For there was I when Lynn confirmed the truth
that she and I could still be orphans yet.

Then, on the bridge, Saint Vitus saw me dance
and Deni too, in nineteen twenties style.
The chance then came for me to swell the ranks
of church folk likewise sainted, after trial.
John Paul, the second pope to take that name,
was quite a man, so many people say.
Was he a saint? If so, what miracles
did he perform? I ask you, if I may.
Now JP2 and I were friends of old,
at least we shared a photograph in Rome,
so as I touched the polished plaque that day
I asked for health to be restored at home.

A clock to time the stars and entertain
the gathered crowd strikes up to forty three.
And, from above, the rooftops view is grand,
like seeing Florence from *Camponile.*
With terracotta tiles on every pitch
and chimneys, smokeless now, give stark relief.
the overall effect is something grand
with Disney images beyond belief.
There is no need to overwork the lungs
by breathless climbing sixty steps to it.
A glass-walled elevator does the work
within a winding staircase, for the fit.

This ancient tower's walls are modern framed,
with steel and concrete columns for the weight.
When was it built and what kept it aloft
until surveyors brought it up to date?
With spiralled steel like triple DNA
right at the core, the elevator car
first rises once then rises once again,
the upper part transparent, like a jar.
An Irish pub for lunch, a carriage ride,
then market stalls for gifts to take away.
The New World by Dvorak, played at home,
a week well spent, and capped by C & A.

*First published in a shorter form as a prize-winning entry
in Quantum Leap magazine May 2008.*

122

You have read that by mid-October 2007 it had became clear to me that the pain and general malaise of which my father had been complaining for several months had far more serious implications than the need for a hip replacement. For some time in the late 1980s and early 1990s he had suffered from pain which became acute from time to time, until he was given a replacement hip joint on his left side.

One day in 1991 I took him, along with Denise, Andrew and Catherine, on a day trip to London which is remembered as one of my fabled whistle stop tours; I once gave Denise a complete guided tour of the Isle of Wight in 2½ hours. On the London trip we saw all the usual sights from the comfort of my car and had the added bonus of seeing Mick Hucknall and Princess Michael of Kent, separately, in chauffeur driven cars trying to pass in the opposite direction in heavy traffic. Mick nodded acknowledgement of our recognition; her ladyship did not! We stopped a little further on, near Ealing, for refreshment and for a toilet break. Apart from that, the whole day was spent in the car and Dad's hip began to seize up. It was hard to get him back into the car after the toilet break and next to impossible to get him out of the car and up the steep driveway to our house in Halesowen a little later. He was in agony!

The surgery was a great success and he enjoyed many active years of dancing, driving and holidaying after it. Inevitably, the other hip, being precisely the same age as the first one and having had more or less the same amount of usage (probably a bit more actually as Dad didn't kick with the left foot in any sense) began to cause problems and Dad started to feel similar pangs of pain which, before the end of August 2007, rendered him virtually house-bound.

This time the pain seemed to start in his right hip and to radiate upwards. The fact that the pain from the left hip had radiated downwards, as was logical, did not give Dad cause to suspect that there might be a fundamental difference, at least that is what he said. I doubt if I shall ever the know full detail of the events leading up to his final illness but I do know that before I left for that short holiday in Prague, Dad and I came as close as we had ever been to having cross words when he accused me of being just one more person who refused to believe him when he said that all he needed was another hip replacement. Of course neither I nor any of my co-accused had anything other than his best interests in mind when we expressed the need for more widespread and intensive investigations but in response to his typically gentle but definite suggestion that I may have (still unimaginable) ulterior motives, I stated that I had no wish to become an orphan. In the state of mind to which he had been driven by pain and worry he was initially unable to accept the concept of a man in his late middle age being an orphan but the penny eventually dropped and peace reigned once more. We tacitly agreed that it was possible but neither expected it to come about as soon as it did.

My mother had died seventeen years earlier, without warning (at least not to me) one December night after heavy snow had prevented a visit to her for a few days previously. Her death happened too quickly to think about and, afterwards, there was still Dad and the family house to create the illusion that things hadn't changed irretrievably.

My great great grandfather, William, lived to be 93 and I always said to Dad that he would have to break that record by reaching 94. That would have been in November 2018 and the resultant party would also have encompassed the centenary of the end of the Great War. Denise's late father, Ernie, was born on Boxing Day 1918 so we would have raised a glass to his posthumous centenary too. Irene, another direct descendant of William, had already beaten his record for longevity but then I had not as yet had the pleasure of her acquaintance.

Although baptised into the Anglican Church, or at least **in an** Anglican church, Dad spent most of his life as a Methodist and it was fitting that within minutes of his death, a few words of prayer were spoken over his body by a Methodist Minister. She was a delightful lady and a dear friend so my sister Lucy, Denise and I were all grateful that it was she who was there to perform this 'last rite' and she found some very lovely and fitting words, whilst ending with the statement that he was now 'flying with angels'. As Dad had spent his last few weeks pain-deadened with morphine, he had been known to be disorientated on occasions, and was sometimes totally bewildered as to where he was and what day it was. We had come to refer to this state of mind with fondness as his being 'away with the fairies' and so the Minister's words had a sort of resonance for us that I am quite sure she did not intend.

Dad's passing has given me food for thought in many ways, including reflections of our life together not just since Mom's death, after which we certainly had many more conversations, but also, and indeed more significantly, during the earlier years.

124

As a child I was precocious, as a teenager I was rebellious, and as a young man I was arrogant. Some will say that I am still arrogant as an old man and they would probably be correct but (perhaps as evidence of that view) I am less concerned about that than I am about the heartache that I must have caused to both of my parents during my teens and early twenties when I still lived at the family home with them but spent every single evening 'socialising' in one way or another.

More often than not I would return well after midnight if at all and they must have been enormously worried, especially as I was usually in my car and had been known to frequent licensed premises from time to time! I would like to think that I gave both of them some pleasure and possibly some pride during their lives but I fear that any such compensations fell miserably short of the sadnesses, the embarrassments and the worries that I undoubtedly caused them to suffer. I wish I had been more thoughtful but am I the only recent orphan to have such feelings of remorse? I suspect not but that does not make it right.

Anyone reading this who is still blessed with two natural parents alive, not to mention any step-parents who in my experience are often the complete opposite of the 'Cinderella' model, please listen and learn. Love them and let them know you do before it is too late. The nearest I got to that was telling Dad on my 50th birthday that I could not have done what I had in life without him. I didn't even manage that much with Mom, I never thought!

'Thoughtless' is another vehicle for expressing these regrets.

Thoughtless

I never thought that I would be
an orphan, all alone.
I never thought that I would see
the day when hope was gone.

I never thought that Mother's heart
would fail that frozen night.
I never thought that was the start
of sorrow at its height.

I never thought that Dad would die
at less then ninety four.
I never thought that he would fly
with angels evermore.

I never thought that either one
could fret or be concerned.
I never thought but, now they're gone,
it's clear I never learned

I never thought!

Bearing in mind my father's connections to the Methodist Church, there could never have been any doubt about the fact that he would have a funeral ceremony with a religious theme. The only questions were as to where it should be held and who should conduct it.

In theory, Dad was a member of one particular church and indeed he attended services there regularly and frequently. However, he had made it clear to me many times that he regarded another church as his spiritual home, having been an even more regular and more frequent visitor there until his interest in my mother as a future wife led him to her church. Over the next fifty years, first one building and then another that housed her church was condemned as being beyond economic repair and so the building that was in use at the time of Dad's death, as it happens also the nearest in the circuit to where he lived, was quite remote from his original roots.

I was still contemplating the relative merits of each when my sister reminded me of some views that our mother had expressed on the subject of her own funeral many years earlier. She did not want her coffin to be wheeled or carried into church for a service then out again to be taken to the crematorium for another ceremony before committal. The decision was therefore easy to make; the service would be held at the crematorium. The group of churches, known to Methodists as a circuit, to which those that Dad attended belonged, had a minister who had spent some time with Dad during his last few weeks of life in addition to the lady mentioned earlier who was on hand to bless him before he had in fact been certified as dead by the doctor.

We had no wish to offend either by asking the other to officiate and, in any event, we were very aware of the fact that neither actually knew him very well at all. One thing about Methodist ministers is that they are a transient bunch, rarely being allowed to stay in one place more than a handful of years and therefore being institutionally incapable of developing any appreciation of life-long relationships that straddle generations.

At a memorial service held for my mother a week or two after her funeral, the keynote speech, or eulogy if you will, was beautifully delivered by Mrs. Ivy Round-Hancock whose father, David Round, had actually been involved in Mom's baptism over sixty years earlier. I was a guest at his 80th birthday party in 1969. Ivy's daughter and I are also friends, and it is that depth of knowledge and bonding, which takes a century or more to develop, that the 'professionals' cannot possibly provide.

What is more, Dad's life in its final decade or so had changed out of all recognition to the one that Lucy and I knew and loved him by and we were gravely concerned that well meant speeches from newcomers would exclude all reference to his early life of which they could not have had any real knowledge.

Fortunately, our mother has a surviving sibling who happens to be a lay preacher on the same circuit. To our delight, our Uncle Norman agreed to conduct Dad's funeral and he did so with enormous sensitivity but with full appreciation of the most substantive parts of Dad's life using a knowledge base built up over the 60 years that they knew each other well. As part of the ceremony, he asked me to deliver an address. Not an easy task, but one from which I would never shrink. I spoke of how Dad was my hero, and the less obvious reasons why, before reading a poem I had written especially for the occasion. I called it **'Requiem'** with a rare lapse of imagination, possibly comforted by two very imaginative men, Andrew Lloyd Webber and Wolfgang Amadeus Mozart, having similarly named respective works written in similar circumstances. The words need no explanation as I am sure they are those that most could, or at least would, write about their own fathers. The basic fact is that Dad never let me down when I was child, nor when I was a very difficult adolescent, nor even when I was a, slightly less difficult, family man in my own right. I told his still, wasted form all of that a few minutes after his death and I thanked him for all he had done for me.

'Requiem', together with the short speech that preceded it at his funeral, was my way of telling everyone else.

To conclude the chapter, there was also some slight difficulty in arranging a memorial service for Dad, again because of professional resistance. Bearing in mind my general thoughts on popes and saints, I could see some merit in their view that a church service should not be allowed to take on the look of 'Dennis Woodall, This is Your Life'. For once, the wishes of the congregation prevailed and a wonderful eulogy was delivered by Dad's dear friend for 70 years, Jack Neale.

Requiem

What was my father, what was he to me?
What role did he fulfil to shape my life?
What guidance issued forth to help me see?
What comforts came from him in times of strife?

When I was hungry, did he give me food?
When I was desperate has he helped me pay?
When I was restless could he change my mood?
When I was lost did he show me the way?

How many times was transport given free?
How many indiscretions were ignored?
How often did my father rescue me?
How often was he both my shield and sword?

The answers to all these were never sad.
They were all positive so 'Thank you, Dad'

The title of my earlier book, *'Out of the Shadow'* was inspired by a line from a poem lamenting the losses of the Great War but that it specifically referred to the way I have felt since the death of my father.

The first shadow across my world had its origins in the death of Archduke Franz Ferdinand, a man with an impressive title and with every expectation of inheriting several even more impressive ones before long. Indirectly, his death came to cause misery to millions and chaos to the world order that existed at the time. I have designated my father's death as 'the second shadow' but only because that is how us poets talk; the truth is of course that there have been many shadows across my world over the years, including illness and death of numerous close relatives and dear friends. Somehow an opening line of 'A three hundred and twenty seventh shadow falls across my life' doesn't really work so I settled for the 'second shadow' at the expense of accuracy.

My father never had a title, other than Mister and various ranks when he was in the Army and the Boys' Brigade, but I do remember he and my uncles referring to each other as 'Squire' back in the 1950s and 1960s. This was presumably a term of endearment akin to 'Mate', 'Sport', 'Blade', 'Son', 'Pal', 'Chum', 'Old Cock' and numerous other such names that I have used for close colleagues over the years.

The poem which follows, another sonnet, needs little further explanation, it is another lament for my father but also for my mother whose funeral we arranged in the same Undertaker's room that we did for Dad seventeen years later, to the day - 10th December. After her death Dad was still there to cover for her, as it were, but with his death the lights really did grow dim for me and I think for my sister too. The shadow will never go away but perhaps, in time, younger members of our family will generate enough light for it to become less oppressive. They are doing their best already, just by existing.

The first line of *'Shadows'*, as with the titles of both previous books, has its origins in my earlier poem. However, I drew on the first line of one of Wilfred Owen's best poems for my last line, as I am sure you will recognise as it is one of my all time favourites.

Shadows

A second shadow falls across my life
and others' too, but not the world-wide mess
the Archduke's death once left, and all the strife.
This passing of a squire a sweet sadness.

The sweetness comes from more than fifty years
of memories, mixing happy times with sad.
The feeding, teaching, caring, quelling fears
essential presents for this learning lad.
The fear returns once more as Christmas nears
and takes the truest friend I ever had.

That feast-time phantom came to us before
to bear away dear Mother, not yet old.
Her light then coming from the torch Dad bore
but now for him those passing bells are tolled.

I think it was Emile Ford who, when I was first interested in popular music, warbled on about hurting people close to you just because you love them. The singer, or his mushy song-writer, was talking about an entirely different kind of love to that which I refer but, in my considerable experience, the same applies at least as much to close blood relatives.

It will be clear to the reader by now, and I am not out of the shadow yet, that my father's death was the worst thing that has happened to me to date. This bold statement does by no means diminish the pain I felt at the death of my mother in 1990 but it does feel worse than that did and I am still not totally sure why that should be. After all, for the first forty years (nearly) of my life I would have said that I was closer to Mom than I was to Dad.

However, I do feel more comfortable when I have explanations for things – Mom was usually able to provide these, incidentally – and so far I think that there are at least three contributory factors.

1.   I was still just about in my thirties when Mom died, whereas I was nearer to sixty than any other milestone birthday when Dad died and therefore much more aware of my own mortality.

2.   There was the 'role model thing'.

        As I said at Dad's funeral, he was a hero figure for me when I was a lad because he had dark, wavy hair like Ronnie Allen, Richard Greene and other heroes, whereas mine was straight and blond. He could repair anything from a Vespa gearbox to a Goblin Teasmade, he could sing, he used to play football (actually I may have gone too far there, he was only a goalkeeper!) and he was popular with everyone. What an impossible act to follow!

3.   He was the last of my parents to die.

When Mom died he was there to take on her role as well as his own; she would have done the same if their departures had been in the reverse order.

Having said that, I'm not at all sure that she could have changed the 13 amp plug on a hair dryer never mind do a full day's work, have dinner (or tea as we called it then) strip the engine of an 850cc Mini, re-grind the valve seatings and renew the cylinder head gasket and then put it all back together in time for me to go up the pub in it for the last couple of pints before closing time. That is exactly what Dad did once, in 1973.

Of course I don't mean that she would literally have taken on his role, just that she would have enabled us, as he did, to carry on for another seventeen years under the partial delusion that nothing actually life-changing had happened.

In *'Contagion'* I have cast his death in the role of a terrible and infectious virus that he had brought into our family, unwittingly and unintentionally, hurting the ones he dearly loved, just by dying!

I use the word 'House' in the dynastic sense, as words like 'clan' and 'tribe' are both too alien-sounding and 'family' has too many syllables.

Contagion

You always hurt the one you love,
how right that singer was.
But did he realise how well
the words describe this loss?

With singers and with poets too,
such words come from the heart.
But now for me the head knows best,
when will this pain depart?

One near and dear may catch a germ
then pass it on to us.
That is the way that illness spreads
in shops or on the bus.

But there is yet another ill
that can infest our nest.
A virus left to us, of which
we cannot soon divest.

Its name is sorrow, or distress,
its symptoms linger long.
Pray one day shall our House be clear
to hear a joyful song.

I really haven't bothered to check the historic economic facts on this, as they may get in the way of the story and in any event are likely to be boring, but when I was first made aware of the reality that most of us have to work to earn a living, the sum of £1,000 per year was regarded as a reasonable standard to aspire to.

By the time I actually started to earn my own living, at £338 per year, the standard had not lifted very much and a slightly older fellow trainee surveyor with whom I became more friendly about twenty years later was a bit of a role model for my cohort as at the age of only 22 he was earning £1,100 per year and also had the exclusive use of a company car, albeit a basic 850cc Mini.

Then the 1970s happened. The lunatics took over the asylum and lazy, ill-educated, unskilled workers held us all to ransom through the power of unions. Margaret Thatcher eventually sorted the problem out but not before a culture of expectancy had become ingrained into the lives of those never previously capable of achieving such a level of luxury as that to which they had become accustomed.

Nevertheless, the likes of my dear old Dad knew what he still thought of as being his place in the greater scheme of things and continued to take only what he had worked for. He adjusted his arbitrary ceiling of income only in line with inflation. When he retired in 1989 he was just short of breaking through the £6,000 per year barrier although in truth he had spent the last few years doing work (and therefore earning) well below his abilities and training.

He had been made redundant at least twice previously during his working life and when this happened for a third time, as a result of his employers re-locating to another part of the world, he was about sixty and had little chance of finding new employment at a time when unemployment figures were still rising monthly.

It was and still is a young man's world but he did take an unskilled and not very well paid job with a local builder of my acquaintance to fill the time between then and when he officially retired at the age of sixty five.

A regular errand for me to run in the early 1960s was to the butcher for 'a piece of beef about 8 shillings'. After tax, that represented about an hour's work for Dad at the time. We had Sunday lunch (or dinner as we called it then) and an evening snack (which we called supper) off the joint which then provided a pie-filling or a stew for our main meal on Monday. I was never, ever, left hungry.

Although Dad did have a relatively good standard of living for the last twenty years of his life, at least in terms of holidays, cars, eating out and general socialising, he often commented on the fact that he had just fallen short of the £6,000 per year ceiling that he perceived to have existed for him at the time when he left the rat-race of wage slaves. He was completely wrong as, not only did his pensions (State and Company) and his interest on savings give him an income well in excess of that, but also the value of his main asset, our family home, was increasing by nearly that amount on average every single year of his retirement. Dad would never have seen it that way as he was conditioned to the concept of having to work for an hour to earn his Sunday lunch. He died rich beyond not only his wildest dreams but also beyond his real appreciation of how well he had done.

It was a grand achievement which I have summarised in the poem of that name which follows and also with the poem after that, which I believe makes my thoughts on the subject of disposing of the house that Mom and Dad left for Lucy and I quite clear; it was more than our nest, it was our base for half a century and it is very sad to see it now with a large white van parked on the recently widened driveway.

A Grand Achievement

Twenty pounds a week was quite a sum
for a man to earn when I was young.
Twenty two was like the juicy plum
of promotion from the bottom rung.

Aided by inflation in those years
which saw pay go up and up and up,
lifestyles of the worker and his peers
then became an overflowing cup.

But each has a ceiling made of glass
above which he will never tower.
Six times twenty, the figure to pass,
sounds lesser still at three pounds an hour.

The weakness lurks in the strange belief
that income to effort is direct
and forty pence for the Sunday beef
needs an hour of labour to collect.

But when the work is over at last
and the wages come from pension rights,
clever investments made in the past
will maintain the earnings day and night.

Not a bread winner with ready cash,
more a solid, long-term savings plan.
Over twenty years it passed the glass
and the worker died a wealthy man.

Leaving home

When I was a very much younger man
I left the nest that had been made for me,
by those who cared as only parents can,
and flew to one much higher in the tree.
Up there, the branches bend more in the breeze
and sometimes they snap and plummet to earth
but stronger limbs below can support with ease
the falling fledgling, as they did from birth.

Now I am a very much older man
the nest is mine or, at least, one share.
The other is held by Lucy McCann
as we sit secure with our souls laid bare
and try to talk about our future plan
but our thoughts are still of that caring pair.

In the 1960s, youth was everything and everyone either was or wanted to be a pop star; many people, mainly men, now in late middle age, can often be heard to claim that they used to be in a group. For the benefit of any readers under forty-ish, a group is what you might recognise as being a band but please bear in mind that what us older types know as a band would involve a couple of dozen musicians playing instruments that mostly needed blowing rather than twanging and had brass as the most common material.

A similar line up but with a majority of instruments that needed bowing was an orchestra which didn't manoeuvre in the dark or otherwise and which operated just as well with or without electric light.

Even I had a minor involvement with a group known variously as 'Image '66' or 'Buttercream Éclair', as substitute drummer on 'Paint it Black' and doing the recorder bits on 'Semi-detached Suburban Mr. James'. I had been dropped before the group's one and only public appearance was made.

Other than in a Boys' Brigade band, which mainly involved instruments that needed to be bashed while marching up and down, my career as a performing musician was therefore over before I had reached the age of fifteen. However, I had not given up my aspirations as a songwriter and that particular itch was scratched in two ways. I tried to impress girlfriends by writing songs about them, without success either with the songs or the girls and I also helped my younger sister and her friend to further their own ambitions, to become the next Lulu and Cilla Black, by writing their material. I have already confused you my calling my sister Lucy when her name is Lynda but everyone else knows her as Lynn and I can now add that when singing she called herself Beverley Blake. She and Gillian Evitts spent hour after hour rehearsing the 'A' side of their debut single (despite it having been written from the male viewpoint) in Dad's garden shed while I was writing the 'B' side at the piano in the dining room. Both sets of lyrics now follow, having been tweaked slightly to read as poems, albeit very poor ones.

'Why?' was the 'A' side and *'Obsession'* was the 'B' side although both titles only came in at the tweaking stage.

Why?

Why do you walk away each time you see me
and close your ears when I have things to say?
Please don't say that you don't do these things to me
because I saw you only yesterday.

Why do you laugh when I say I dream of you
and each time I ask you to be my wife?
You know that I love the very thought of you
and I'd worship you the rest of my life.

If you've found someone else why don't you tell me
and maybe I would leave you both alone.
If he leaves don't you think of running to me
because then you'll turn round and find me gone.

Why do you walk away each time you see me
and close your ears when I have things to say?
Please don't say that you don't do these things to me
because I saw you only yesterday.

Adapted from a 1969 song called 'As if I didn't know'
written by Graham and Lynda Woodall
and performed by Beverley Blake and Gillian Evitts.

Obsession

You know that I love you
I always think of you.
From night until morning
and morning till night.

And if you should leave me,
refuse to believe me,
I'll always dream of you
till dawn's early light

As soon as the sun dies
just after the moon rise
you'd fill up my thinking
if never in sight.

And during the daytime,
when covered in work grime,
you'd colour my vision
but no black or white.

So stay with me always,
release me from this daze
and spend every moment
just holding me tight.

*Adapted from an untitled 1969 song
written by Graham Woodall*

In 1966, to make way for road-widening or some such municipal nonsense that never materialised, my grandmother, Maud, was forced to sell what had been a family home for over forty years. It was originally called Field House but was, and still is, known affectionately by the family as Number Ten! She was already 78 years old and had seen most members of her family live there at one time or another. Several members of that family, including me, had been born there. She was re-located to a new ground-floor flat nearby, overlooking the church yard that had held her husband, Bert, since 1939 but the stress of the move took its toll on her health and she died just before Christmas 1967. A great deal of belongings had been accumulated over the years and these were either disposed of or shared among her descendants in two tranches – the first at the time of the move and the second immediately after her death. Various trinkets came to me, including a few cuff-links, tie pins and the like, and also several military medals in which I was at that time only slightly interested and of which I had little understanding. I did note that at least one of the medals was inscribed around its edge with the name 'Sperring' but I had absolutely no idea who that was nor did I take the trouble to find out for another forty years!

Like many teenagers, I used to decorate my bedroom walls with all sorts of posters, photographs and general souvenirs and that is where some of the medals were displayed until I left my parents' house for my own in 1977. Some years after that, I became aware that I didn't know what had become of the medals but by then I had moved from one house to another several times and so I was content to assume that they were somewhere in one of the many boxes that had moved with me but had remained unopened for years. I never forgot the medals and I had established that William Sperring was the name of Maud's brother-in-law; husband to her sister, Sarah. William had died in 1925 and Sarah, childless, in 1943 after being nursed at Number Ten by Maud.

Further research provided me with a copy of the medal card of Private W. Sperring of the West Yorkshire Regiment from which I was able to confirm my recollection that he won the War Medal and the Victory Medal. The others that I had acquired were commemorative medallions to mark the fiftieth and sixtieth anniversaries of Queen Victoria's accession to the throne. I was also vaguely aware that my mother had retained one or two similar items which I thought to be duplications of some of those in my care.

Early in 2008, whilst yet again clearing out a family home after the death of a loved one, this time my father, I first discovered that I had in fact left 'my'

142

medals behind when I moved out in 1977 and, second, I found those that had remained in my mother's drawer. By that time I was very much more familiar with the subject and I had in fact acquired a set of replica medals of my own and was toying with the idea of having them engraved with Great Uncle Will's name, rank and number. I was therefore able to recognise immediately that his Victory Medal had been converted, by the brazing on of a pin, to a brooch which I assume his widow, like many others, wore in his honour until her own death. I have had it restored, albeit not quite faithfully, and I have acquired a replacement ribbon for it.

The surprise was that what I had taken to be another Victory Medal, possibly having been awarded to Will's brother James, was actually a German medal of some type! I have enough of the language to translate the inscriptions and to thereby identify it as a similar item to the Jubilee and Diamond Medallions struck in honour of Queen Victoria but having been produced to commemorate the centenary of the birth of the first Kaiser Wilhelm.
I do wonder whether or not my mother was aware of the detail of this strange addition to the collection; perhaps she had kept it hidden for fear of accusations of unpatriotic activity. What I wonder even more is how on Earth such an article came to be in the possession of a steelworker from the Black Country. He had seen service on the Western Front and one is forced to accept the possibility that he took it from the victim of a bayonet charge.

However, it is at least as likely that Will bought it from a fellow Old Soldier for the price of a pint. Either explanation would fit the known facts but it remains a mystery as to why a Front Line German soldier in 1917 or thereabouts would be wearing a medal struck in 1897. Perhaps it was a lucky (sic) charm given to him by his father as he set off for war.

I established that it should have a yellow ribbon and I have found a replacement for that. Was the original ribbon lost in battle or subsequently, or was it left behind like the other half of Kipps's sixpence? The American custom of tying a yellow ribbon around a tree in anticipation of the return of a loved one has become well known in England since the 1973 popular song but was it a pre-1914 German custom too?

Or did a sweetheart wear it in her long blonde hair pending the safe return of her intended? Did she marry another when she learned of his death?

We shall never know the answers to these questions but what is for sure is that my Great Uncle William was not officially the recipient of the Kaiser

143

Wilhelm I Centennial Medal. I call it a 'crown' with allusion to another type of coin, the King's shilling, as well as to the small part Will played in the eventual abdication from the throne of Kaiser Wilhelm II.

Amongst the other items we found were some from my grandparents' early life, one of which was finally considered to be of no further use as recently as July 2008. This was a badly damaged sun-shade and the others were a straw boater and a cane, the like of which one sees in films about the old music hall days, Laurence Olivier's Archie Rice in *'The Entertainer'*, for example. They all belonged to my grandparents and I have a mental image of them strolling in the sun circa 1913 in or near to Farley Park, perhaps on the land upon which her final earthly dwelling place was to be built later, and certainly very close to the piece of land under which they have now lain together for nearly twice as long as they did in life.

To avoid confusion, I should mention at this point that Maud's father was also called William and that I assume that he would not have allowed her to 'walk out' with Bert very far from his shop above which they lived, without a chaperone.

As you will read elsewhere, my grandfather through the medium of my dear mother, left me with some life-defining sayings as well as a genetic hatred of the Labour Party.

My grandmother taught me to read well before I started school, simply by sitting me on her lap and reading to me. I owe them both a great deal. The following two poems, *'The Kaiser's Crown'* and *'Field House findings'* both arise from these and other discoveries made at the house they once shared.

The Kaiser's Crown

Great Uncle Will, what did you do so wrong
to get your hands upon the Kaiser's Crown?
What beaten breast to you gave up its gong
to rest for ninety years among your own?

The gold and silver ones were yours by right,
your name and rank engraved around the side.
But this one, copper-coloured, shining bright
could not be won, no matter how you tried.

And was its yellow ribbon left at home,
tied tight around a tree or in the hair
of a flaxen fraulein who would not roam
until she heard the news she could not bear?

Did Fritz or Gottlieb taste your English steel
before you took a secret souvenir?
Or was the medal your share of a deal
struck back in Blighty with a glass of beer?

Your own Sweet Sarah, with her raven locks,
wore one of your rewards when you were gone.
Its rainbow ribbon left inside the box
with other trophies – howsoever won!

Then after she had met her mortal end,
as did her sister, niece and other kin,
the duty fell to me to mend and tend
those symbols of a prize no-one could win.

And so I shall, for what is left of life
for me upon this Earth, still badly scarred
by your war and all other times of strife
although the Kaiser's Crown's not on your card.

Field House findings

A closet that, for forty years, had held
mementos of the tapestry of life
gave up its goods to those of us too young
to know the time when Maud was once a wife.
On bill-hooks, papers from the past were spiked
and gave us fleeting flashbacks of the days
when she and those before her on her line
were less in fear of municipal ways.

Amidst the bills-of-sale and bric-a-brac
we found three artefacts of bygone years
when Maud went walking out alone with Bert,
perhaps within the range of William's ears.
A swishy stick of cane, a straw-brimmed hat
and, last of all, a sun-bleached parasol
gave glimpses of a pre-war holiday
from shops and steel onto a quiet knoll.

The hat and cane did not survive the move,
unless folk tell me different by and by,
the pretty parasol was nice to keep
in another closet, but who knows why?
A gamp it was to Maud, as in a tale
that was still fairly fresh when so was she,
but just a battered brolly it became
so, with a heavy heart, I set it free.

Not much remains of Bert and Maud today,
except our flesh and blood, but I am part
of that genetic heritage of course,
perhaps I also have a dodgy heart.
But other legacies were left to me
by Nan and Granddad, I am proud to say,
his were the words of wisdom that I have
and hers the gift of reading every day.

First published as a prize-winning entry in Quantum Leap Issue 44 November 2008

Throughout my childhood there was mention within the family of an ancestor of ours who was the first man in West Bromwich to own a motor car. There was also a photograph of the man in his car which I assumed had been taken during one of his visits to our branch of the family. In comparatively recent years, I came to realise that the man in question was actually the grandfather of my own grandmother, Maud, and that his name was Thomas Gibbons. I also realised that no house in the family looked like the one in the picture and in any event it would have been unlikely that we would have had a camera ready to take such a picture. Then, during one of my periodic spells of family research, I found a cousin called Thomas Gibbons or, to be more accurate, he found me. We soon became friends and he supplied me with lots of information on the Gibbons branch of my family and also introduced me to his father, Paul.

For almost two decades I lived in the Hill Top area of West Bromwich and although I had always known that my Gibbons ancestors had been based there in the early years of the 20th century, I didn't know exactly where until Tom showed me one of the houses, still standing, a few yards below the Sow and Pigs public house. I could never begin to count the number of times I have walked or driven past that house during my lifetime but I estimate that it must be in excess of ten thousand.

I learned that I am descended from Thomas's first wife but that he had two more who also predeceased him and that all of them were buried in the cemetery at the top of Heath Lane. Thomas was what we might describe as a mechanical engineer and in the late 1890s he had taken out a patent on some process of metal component manufacture which appears to have been the source of his sizeable fortune.

The car turns out to have been made by the Star Motor Company of Wolverhampton and we think that the photograph may have been taken at the rather grand home of one of the owners of that company. While lying in hospital bed in Wolverhampton in February 2010 , almost certainly very close to where the car was made and where the photograph was actually taken, I passed the time by writing a poem about my illustrious great great grandfather. To distinguish him we now refer to him as *'Star Car Thomas'* and I have given the poem the same name.

Star Car Thomas

He's known as Star Car Thomas now
by those of us who love him.
A hundred years ago The Sow
and Pigs stood just above him.

The first man in my town of birth
to own a horseless carriage
seems to have had substantial girth
and three attempts at marriage.

For, sadly, he lost all his wives,
each taken by the Reaper.
They all have stones to mark their lives
though one or two were cheaper.

With Old Queen Vic still on the throne
our Thomas earned a patent
and fortunes we have not since known
were there, but sometimes latent.

For ninety years his family
would hardly know each other
but then fulfilled the destiny
of William and his brother.

An epigram, as far as I am concerned, is a very short poem which, almost without exception, has to rhyme to make it instantly recognisable as a poem, and which must also contain a message of some sort. Some 'sayings' which may equally be described as proverbs are in fact epigrams as well. 'A stitch in time saves nine' is one example although you will have noticed that there is not exactly a rhyme there but there is just a touch of assonance.

I have no idea about the level of flatulence from which my maternal grandfather may have suffered but a short poem that he used to quote which started 'Let wind go free wherever you be' might offer us a clue. A few of my own will follow soon. Epigrams I mean. I believe that Granddad was actually quoting from an epitaph to someone who died of wind!

In the early 1970s I had a work colleague who was also a bit of a philosopher and who treated me to the benefit of his worldly wisdom on a number of subjects. At one stage, I was working my way through what for me was a particularly tricky piece of coursework in my struggle to qualify as a surveyor and I was particularly puzzled by the art of valuation; there is NO WAY that it is a science! At the same time I was having almost daily arguments with one party or another as to the price of construction work, as opposed to the cost of it or to the value of it, which are three different things and all are outside the scope of this book. My wise friend told me simply that both the value and the cost of anything is fixed according to the circumstances but the price of anything is no more and no less than the amount that someone will pay for it. I still had to read all the books, and then regurgitate the right stuff onto my examination papers, but the principle of what he said was clear and sound and I have followed it faithfully for about thirty five years now, although for professional reasons I have to do the calculations and comparables as well. *'Valuations'* is the epigram that grew out of this.

I stated earlier that a short poem has to have rhymes or else there will not be enough of it to be recognised as a poem. I immediately followed this with the exception to prove the rule but what I mean is that not just any short statement could be regarded as an epigram. With longer pieces of writing the distinction is less clear cut; many poems, not just modern ones, don't have rhymes at all. Others have no regularity of metre or line length but with clever use of other poetic devices, such as alliteration to name but one, they sneak under the wire and appear in books of poems.

In extreme but not rare cases, what may well be well-written, clever and even beautiful prose is subjected to indiscriminate vivisection to create new

149

lines at random places in the text. I have no idea why writers do this and I can only put it down to silliness. Free verse, however is something different and is, I suspect, what such writers are actually seeking to achieve. I have written several pieces myself in this style but, even then, I could never see what a new line would achieve that a comma or full stop would not, other than the overall appearance of the page. Perhaps that really is all that there is to it. Anyway, **'Poetry and Prose'** is my epigram on the matter.

Other forms of poetry, with very rigid rules about metre and line length are no better, to my taste, although the brevity of most of these forms does lend itself to epigrams. One of the newest of these forms is called **'Tetractys'** which uses the 1, 2, 3, 4, 10 formation. Mathematically balanced $(1 + 2 + 3 + 4 = 10)$ and thereby with its attractions for me but still it not exactly a favourite form of poetry so I wrote an epigram in that form to poke a little fun at it. Measured in terms of line length it goes from constipation to diarrhoea over its five lines.

The **'Urban myth'** comes from a 1961 pop song by Johnny Tillotson but readers may infer, from the foregoing comments and from others made later, another meaning. Who knows?

EPIGRAMS

Valuations

The worth of a lot
is the worth it has got.
But the price of a thing
is the price it will bring.

Poetry and Prose

The rhymes and chimes
let chopped up prose
develop into poetry.
But strings of words
without all those
are only verses, loose but free.

Tetractys

This
form of
poetry
is nothing more
than verbal irritable bowel syndrome.

Urban myth

The singer sang with flawed devotion,
there is no poetry in motion!

I wrote at some length in **'Across my World'**, and added more in the sequel, about my discovery and reunion of both friends and family members as a result of modern communication systems, including the internet. I have also paid tribute to the work of my cousin, Brian Woodall, in tracing our family tree back to the 16th century along several branches. With the advent of computer technology we have been able to add breadth to the direct lines and I have found many 'cousins' as a result of this. There is more about this topic later but, for now, I will tell you about a truly astonishing revelation that was made to me by one such distant cousin, Frances Castle. It happened by chance. Frances is my relation on what I shall call 'the Woodall side' although none of her ancestors carried that name. As such we have a common ancestor in Isabel Sherwin, but Sherwin is also a name on Frances's mother's side and it was for that reason that she was researching it. To her astonishment, and then to mine, it emerged that Isabel was the niece of Ralph Sherwin who, as any good Roman Catholic will tell you, was a thorn in the side of Queen Elizabeth I. He was born in Rodsley, Derbyshire in 1550, the son of John Sherwin and Constance (neé Woodward), one of several children including a brother named John to whom I shall return shortly. Ralph was educated at Eton College and then Exeter College, Oxford where he took a Master of Arts degree on 2nd July 1574. Over four hundred years later, I was to discover that my friend and colleague, Brian Polley, also had an M.A. from Exeter College. At that stage Ralph was still of the Protestant faith but he converted to Roman Catholicism in 1575, became a bishop in 1577 and went to Rome soon afterwards for three years. In 1580 he returned to England but after six months or so he was arrested and imprisoned but continued his mission by converting fellow inmates and so he was transferred to the Tower of London where he was tortured on the rack. There is a strong but not entirely proven story that Queen Elizabeth I offered to create him an Archbishop, second only to Canterbury if he would only renounce his new faith and return to being a Protestant. I realise, of course, that at that time and for another century or so beyond it was something of a gamble to declare for one side or the other when it came to the power struggle between Protestants and Roman Catholics in England; back the wrong horse in that particular race and you would be more likely to lose your head than your proverbial shirt. My Uncle Ralph was clearly reading the wrong form book, possibly seeing Elizabeth growing old without issue and expecting her to die or be overthrown within the foreseeable future and to be replaced by a Roman Catholic monarch. It could have gone either way but, perhaps only with the benefit of four centuries of hindsight, it is clear to me that he made the wrong choice. He may as well have gone straight to the stables of the Four Horsemen of the Apocalypse because the next few months of his life were like Hell on Earth and eventually led to Judgement Day for him and his friend, Edmund Campion, with them being tried for treasonable conspiracy and found guilty. Ralph was hanged, drawn and quartered at Tyburn on 1st December 1581, the first member of the English College in Rome to become a martyr. Having been beatified in 1886, Ralph was made a saint in 1970, the year I became eligible to vote and Edward Heath became Prime Minister, possibly a coincidence. Returning to his brother, John, he had a son, William, who had a daughter, Isabel. For many years we have known about Isabel who married Francis Sadler and had a son, also called William. In turn, young William married Esther Tabberer and had a daughter called Ann who married Samuel Porter in 1715 or thereabouts. Two more Samuel Porters followed in successive generations in a direct line until a girl of the line, Mary, married John Phipps in about 1815. I am in contact with members of the Porter family, principally Kenneth who was born in 1925 and who has lived in Seattle for over half a century. He was both pleased and surprised to hear about our close connection to Saint Ralph although I don't think that he is any more of a Roman Catholic than I am.

At the risk of sounding as if I have now moved back from the Book of Revelations to the Book of Genesis, I shall continue with the genealogy........

John and Mary Phipps begat (a Genesis word if ever there was one) Louisa who later married John Smith (every family has one) and had a daughter whom they called Evelyna. By this stage we are starting to see names that become repeated in later generations although the next Evelyna did not reach adulthood. The Evelyna who forms part of my direct line married George Slater and gave life to my great grandmother, Louisa. This Louisa is the earliest-born member of my family that I actually met, as our lives overlapped by about four years. She was still living in Derby at that time. Throughout this procreation process, shared about equally along mother to daughter lines as along father to son lines and therefore necessitating several name changes, the Woodall line was developing quite straightforwardly from Radulphus who was born in Wistow circa 1560, through ten generations and a distance of about three miles, to Walter who was born in Selby in 1863. You will read elsewhere about subsequent family travels but it is sufficient to say here that whilst at least one of his brothers, another William, went north, Walter went south and settled in Derby where he met and married Louisa Slater.

I started to write the following poem, *'Uncle Ralph'*, in Latin, as befits the subject, and may try again to do so one day. I switched to English for speed and now only the first line of Latin has been retained, as a sub-title.

Uncle Ralph

Ecce! Radulphus Santus in gloria caelestis sedet

Behold! Saint Ralph in heavenly glory sits,
made whole again, from Earthly tortures freed.
His Derby days, combined with those in Rome,
led to the Tower of London for his creed.

From Sherwin stock sprang forth a direct line
as brother John, through Bill, made Isabel.
Her husband was a Sadler and their son
gave Esther Tabberer another girl.
And she, in time, went to the Porter pack
which has Seattle sons in present days.
But after five score years they joined with Phipps
then Smith then Slater then the Woodall phase.

So, Uncle Ralph, that makes you nine times great
to me, a nephew many times removed.
Since your time we have taken different faiths
but even now they all remain unproved.
Exeter College, Oxford, honoured you
Master of Arts. Four hundred years and more
before I met another styled the same,
our World nine times removed from days of yore.

Did Good Queen Bess suggest a bishopric
or was that just a tease to make you wince?
The horse you backed came from Apocalypse
to take you to a See that makes no sense.
The start of Advent fifteen eighty one
came after months of torture on the rack
till you and Brother Edmund left this Earth.
They hung you then your bodies they did hack.

As I became an adult, with a vote,
your Brothers canonised you at long last.
I beg you, Saintly Uncle, hear me now
and greet me when my mortal life has passed.

It is very rare that I get commissioned to write a poem but next we have another of those rare exceptions. After reading an earlier work, my sister-in-law Yvonne asked me to write a poem about her and so I did.

By the time Denise and I arrived in Lichfield, Yvonne and her family, as refugees from Birmingham, had been established here for many years and so we had ready-made friendly neighbours from the start. She will probably not thank me for announcing it to the World but Yvonne is a few years older than I am although a stranger would never guess that as she has no grey hair, lovely smooth skin and all her own teeth, at least as far as I know. She is also a veritable dynamo and the life and soul of every party. Walking and cycling present no difficulties for her and she would pass without question for a woman ten to fifteen years younger.

For a long period of time, when work, football, family and other social commitments permitted, Denise and I would often meet Yvonne and her husband Steve at one of the pubs in Lichfield on Saturday afternoon for a drink before returning to their house or ours for a meal and maybe even a second glass of wine. Despite my natural aversion to dancing, that second glass sometimes lowered my inhibitions far enough to induce me to strut my stuff to whatever music the two sisters had belting out of the stereo at the time. As often as not the work of the late Billy Fury featured somewhere in the evening's programme but Yvonne was equally comfortable with the likes of Michael Jackson and the top Irish act of the day, The Corrs, whom we went to see in concert at the NEC Arena.

However, all good things come to an end and Yvonne and Steve went to live in Spain where they had more sunshine but much less of most other things so, after five or six years, they returned and now live within walking distance so our partying can resume.

The title of the poem says everything there is to say about it, we are back to the sonnets!

155

A Shakespearean Sonnet for a Lady of Spain

Yvonne, my love, a sister dear to me
Your laughing face, lit by youthful vigour
Your caring heart laid bare for all to see
Your feelings fired by a feather trigger

We have laughed and lived and then laughed again
We have drunk and danced and then drunk some more
We have seen the sun and have rued the rain
We have been to a show to see The Corrs

Now you reside in a Spanish villa
Never to meet me in a bar in town
No late night bopping to Jackson's Thriller
Nor gory expletives before each noun

For you have gone to your sunnier clime
Free, with your friends, what a wonderful time!

I have reached that stage of life at which there is a general assumption that if I am not already a grandfather then I shall become one before too long. So far, I have only reached the next milestone back from that by having become a great uncle. My niece, Donna, has a beautiful little girl with the charming name of Elise. Elise is the oldest of her generation on that particular bloodline of the family and she has already been joined by Thomas, Todd, Harriet and George.

By virtue of marriage I have other nieces, one of which is Clare (née Hanson). After a very long courtship, Clare married Pete Rawlings in Hong Kong early in 2005 and having then re-located to Sydney, Australia she was blessed with a daughter in 2007. This little miss is called Rebecca and during a visit to Lichfield in 2008 Clare and Pete decided to have a naming ceremony for her at the Registry Office. Now, I had never previously encountered this particular procedure so, for the benefit anyone else equally ill-informed, I can tell you that it is in essence a Christening service in all but name, and is without the accoutrements of any religious denomination or faith. In point of fact, any reference to religion in the ceremony is prohibited.

As she lives on the other side of the planet we see very little of Rebecca but she brings a smile to my face daily through the medium of a photograph we keep on a shelf in our conservatory. The expression on her face prevents me looking at it without smiling. I was as surprised as I was honoured to be asked to play a small part in the ceremony by reading out a poem that I wrote for Rebecca about the day she was born which, according to the time of day, may well have been a different date for her than it was for us. Wherever I happen to be in the World I regard it as having false time, my body clock is permanently set at English Time.

Up to the time of writing, Rebecca has probably clocked up as many air miles and visited as many different countries I have over the last thirty or forty years but she is really English and I am sure that she will eventually call England her home. She has also acquired a little brother, Ben, who I have recently met and who may well give rise to another poem one day. Throughout my time at Grammar School I was nicknamed Benny or Ben for short and so Denise and I now say that this new addition is called Benny after Uncle Graham, with allusion to Trigger's comments on Del Boy's baby in **'Only Fools and Horses'**

For Rebecca

G'day and welcome to the world
our precious, new-born Sheela.
Rebecca, to be more precise,
of happiness the dealer.

Enough Antipodean slang,
though better that than Canton.
Your origins are England's own
you are, in part, a Hanson.

The letters of your name declare
the standard of your making.
The double R stood for Rolls Royce
and quality past faking.

But now they're yours to take through life,
your Rawlings genes will carry
you to the far flung parts of Earth,
for years you may not tarry.

And then at last you'll come to see
the land of all your forebears.
You may go back, you never know,
or stay to raise your own heirs.

This day is yours but not ours yet,
the international dateline
puts us behind you for a while
as to your health we drink wine.

In North Yorkshire there is a tiny village called Wistow. Since the middle 1960s, thanks to the work of my cousin Brian, I have been aware that it was in this village that our earliest known (and named) ancestors lived. I discovered in more recent years that records even earlier than the ones that Brian used are in existence, having originated in the parish church of All Saints. The dates of founding of both the church and of the village are less than certain but the former is probably as old as English Christianity itself and the latter about the same or even slightly earlier, as the name is from the Danish for 'a wet place' and undoubtedly started as what we would refer to generically as a Viking settlement. Unfortunately, these earlier records are indecipherable now: not because they are written in Latin, although they are, but because they are faded and illegible. These date back to 1315 but there are records of Vicars being based at the Church from much earlier times. What is very clear from the readable records is that the name 'Woodall' is repeated constantly. This is quite enough, when added to the physical appearance of many members of my family, some blond, some very tall and some both, to satisfy me that on my father's side, I am a Viking.

In 1973, I decided to spend a few days on holiday visiting the area, perhaps finding some living distant relatives or at the very least finding some gravestones of departed relatives. I had travelled just over one mile in that direction when I changed my mind and headed my Volkswagen Beetle for the more familiar south-west. It was to be almost thirty years before I finally made it to Wistow and I immediately regretted leaving it so long. As I drove into the village, I passed the Church on my left and looked for somewhere safe to park whilst I explored the graveyard and the Church itself. A spot was found a few yards further on and as I stepped out of the car the first thing that I saw was a street sign which read 'Woodall Court'. This turned out to be a small development of modern houses built on land that used to belong to a much older house which remains and which, I was later informed, was occupied until fairly recent times by a Mrs. Woodall, the last of that name (presumably gained by marriage in her case) to live in Wistow. A tiny empire perhaps, but one that had lasted a thousand years or more! Setting aside, as we must, those ancestors for whom we have no names and no detail but of whose existence there can be no doubt, our earliest forebear was a man called Radulphus who was born about 1560. He had a son called Nicholas who in turn had a son whom he named after Radulphus. At this point I should make it clear that Radulphus, which is the Latin version of Ralph, is not the Sainted member of another branch of my family about whom I have written elsewhere.

The second Radulphus had a son called Robert who, less generously to his father than to his son, (as far as my direct line is concerned) named that offspring after himself, an act repeated in the next generation of this direct line, thereby making three Roberts in a row. Robert the Third named his son Mathew and the old sequence was restored when Mathew called his son William, whose own son was then called Mathew, whose own son became another William when he was born in 1833. In the churchyard there are several headstones that bear the family name, carved in stone, and on the World War I memorial alongside an ancient tree which was planted, we are told, by the older Mathew as a Churchwarden or Sexton, there is the name again. I was told by a lady who looks after the Church that lights are put in that tree every Christmas as part of the festivities. The second Mathew was the last of my line to have been born in Wistow as, after marrying Susannah Dale in nearby Bolton Percy in 1832, he made the giant leap to Selby – a distance of all of three miles. Both he and Susannah are buried in Selby and a headstone to them remains although my efforts to restore and preserve it have so far been unsuccessful. It is of a soft sandstone and whilst the inscriptions are still clearly legible, the expert advice is that weathering is inevitable with time, whatever we try to do. I am not totally convinced and I intend to do what I can to postpone the inevitable. Their son William and his wife Christiana are also buried there in an unmarked grave although the position of the plot is recorded on a plan. I am also considering the erection of a suitably annotated headstone for them. I am in regular contact with some direct descendants of those from the first Mathew onwards, not just those on my direct line, and have also met and become close to several of them. I must therefore seek the agreement of equal relatives before I take any such action although I do not anticipate any objections. Two of the sons of William and Christiana carried the names of William (the 'alternate naming' custom being abandoned again as far as my line is concerned) and Walter. William left Selby and headed north, explained in more detail elsewhere, and Walter headed south to Derby where he married Louisa Slater. Their offspring included another Walter, who was grandfather to Tina, Alfred who was father to Brian and Harold who was father to my father, Dennis. Together with a few other members of the family, also detailed elsewhere, Tina, Brian and I, and recently some of our own children, meet regularly if not exactly frequently in the hope, if not in any great expectation, that the Woodalls will continue to do so in the memory of those from Wistow for another thousand years.

There had to be a poem, didn't there? Here it is and it's called *'Wistow'*.

Wistow

On, past the church and round the bend
there is a court that bears the name.
The name that we shall long append
to Wistow whence our forebears came.

From Radulphus down to Mathew
son after son was settled there.
Some remain, but just the ones who
carefully chiselled stonework wear.

By the tree that we once planted
much taller stonework bears the name.
In that tree, with carols chanted,
the lights rejoice that Jesus came.

In that church all saints are hosted
with our Radulphus, in his time.
Not the one whose banns were posted
but an uncle to our line.

Mathew walked a league to Selby,
grandson Walter went further still.
Married to a girl from Derby,
their tree loves Wistow, always will.

Readers will already be aware of my fascination with World War One in general and the poetry from it in particular. I have even written poems about it myself. The contemporary poetry often painted enduring images of the filth and infestation of the front-line trenches and the terror of imminent death for those trapped in them. Many of the same poems more than hinted at the view that the creatures that shared the trenches with our soldiers were actually preferable to the enemy. Setting aside the ladies at home who thought it somehow clever to give white feathers as emblems of cowardice to any lads of their own ages who had not 'taken the King's shilling' and wore uniforms to prove it, much has been sympathetically written about wives, sweethearts and mothers whose lives were for ever changed by the war and who went through their own form of Hell in many ways. They often had to work in dreadful conditions for very little reward whilst being subject to the constant fear of receiving a telegram bringing the news of the death of a loved one.

Many men, of which my paternal grandfather was one, were prevented from fighting at the front by a ruling that their work in munitions factories was vital to the war effort. They must have been potential targets for the 'white feather brigade' as I have in my possession two certificates issued by respective employers to my grandfather, presumably to carry about his person as a form of defence against any suggestion that he was not 'doing his bit'.

What does not usually appear in anthologies of poetry is sympathy, in their own right, for very young children who may have lost fathers, uncles or older brothers. Scarcer still are poems that deal with the knock-on effect of the war upon the lives of later born relatives of the slaughtered who would never have a grandfather to love, and eventually to mourn, as part of a natural progression.

My great great grandfather, William Woodall, had a large family including two particular sons, William and Walter. Young William had a son called Ernest and Walter had a son called Harold. I have set aside other offspring for the time being, for the sake of clarity. Harold was the grandfather to which I referred above – the bearer of documentary evidence of the importance of his Blighty-based work to the war effort. Ernest, although older than his cousin and by the outbreak of war already a married man with two young daughters, joined the army, fought on the front line and was killed in 1915 close to Ypres. I have seen his name engraved on the Menin Gate.

The younger of his daughters, Winifred, grew up and produced a daughter of her own whom she named Beryl. The older daughter was named Hilda but was always known by her middle name, Irene. Their mother, Ernest's widow, was named Eliza and, left with two children and being still of relatively tender years herself, she re-married. William junior and Walter were both born in Selby but as young adults had both flown the family nest in search of employment. William went north and Walter went south. Travel between Wearside and Derby in the 1880s and 1890s would have made it difficult enough for the brothers to stay in touch and it is distinctly possible that their respective sons never even met. A half-generation age gap between the cousins would have made such a relationship even less likely to have developed and the final chance was lost when Harold moved further South to the munitions factories of the West Midlands and Ernest went to the Western Front.

Ernest's death, Eliza's re-marriage and the 200 miles of separation all combined, I suggest, to keep the two branches of old William's family apart. However, the advent of modern technology allowed me to firstly learn the existence of and subsequently to meet and befriend Ernest's descendants including his daughter Irene whose 99th birthday I was privileged to attend on 16th February 2008, as well as her 100th a year later. Sadly, she died just before reaching the age of 101 so the next family get together was at her funeral. I am in contact with her sons James and John and her grand-daughter Janet as well as with Winifred's daughter Beryl. We all hope to spend some years wining and dining together as our respective forebears should have.

The following poem records this part of our family's history for posterity. The title, *'That stupid war again'*, is another reminder of the less than obvious misery caused by the conflict and this is the reason why I consider that it also affected the likes of people like me whose parents weren't even born for years after it finished.

That stupid war again

Many lines have long been written
of the war to end all wars.
Every poet's flesh was bitten
by the bug that leaves no sores.
Lice and rats and human vermin
were the common things to scorn.
Five nine shells and all things German,
pointless carnage, dusk and dawn.

Safe in Blighty were the ladies
and those men in vital jobs.
All have had their shares of Hades
verbalised with sighs and sobs.
But who wrote about the others,
those still young or not yet born?
Sons and daughters and their brothers
who had no-one known to mourn.

Irene, an Edwardian lady,
lost her father near to Ypres.
Six years old but childhood fading,
as her mother sits and weeps.
Life went on and Mother married.
Why not? She was very young.
Still the Fallen's kinfolk carried
word of him in local tongue.

Ninety years and more went by, all
contact lost with Uncle Walt.
Neither knew the other's trials,
neither had the slightest fault.
Then at last they met like brothers,
Irene there like vintage wine
that Beryl, Janet and the others
drink with Graham and his line.

I wrote earlier of certain young ladies who have comparatively recently become part of my family. There are others; for example my second cousin, Vicky, who is a Woodall by birth, has a daughter by the name of Saskia. Vicky was mentioned in a poem that I included in *'Across my World'* and, when she read it, Saskia expressed disappointment that she had been left out. I therefore resolved to write a poem especially for her by way of compensation. Saskia's younger cousins, Elizabeth and Tom, may demand similar treatment when they are a little older, as may Elise and, if they do, then that will be fine by me.

The inspiration for this piece came from a photograph of Saskia taken in Lichfield's Beacon Park by a friend of Vicky. In it she is hanging upside down from a climbing frame and her long, flame–coloured hair cascades beautifully down, almost reaching the ground. It immediately struck me that she could be the personification of a small space rocket at or just after the point of launching.

As dramatic as the photograph is, I clicked a couple of times with my mouse and looked at it as if she was the right way up. From this angle it looks even more spectacular. As with a lot of my poems, and perhaps even the majority of those written for individuals, this one is of course in sonnet form and the words I have chosen are intended to bring together the differences and, at the same time highlight the similarities, between art and science.

Saskia is a beautiful girl whom any artist from Titian onwards would dearly love to have had as a model. Her aesthetic attributes come from both of her parents in what seem to me to be equal measures and which result in a product that is even greater than the simple sum of the parts. I have attempted to describe such artistic merits in scientific terms, with reference to the works of the man I still think of as the cleverest who ever lived and to various techniques and instruments that one would never expect to see in an artist's studio but might find at the NASA launch site or at mission control.

Let me introduce you now to *'Saskia'*

Saskia

Like forceful flames that give the slender shaped
Saturn 5 its escape velocity
to use the laws of Newton, from the Cape,
her hair thrusts downward in compliancy.
With simpler science I invert the shot,
delete the ground and substitute the sky.
Those flames then flicker upward, fiery hot
but gentle, calm and easy on the eye.

The ice-blue eyes can't hide the warmth within
this other slender shape and kindly face.
Her father's features, joined with other kin
and carried with her mother's style and grace.
It takes no telescope, no search engine
to see this natural beauty in our space.

First published in By the Winter Fires. December 2009

I do have an interest in World War One, its poetry and history in particular can entrance me as would a snake.

I abhor both wars and snakes and I do everything I can to avoid the latter but, with the comfort of knowing it can do me no more harm, I allow myself to be enthralled by the former to the limited extent of the 1914-1918 conflict. I have felt that way for over forty years but it was not until it dawned on me that the world is rapidly running out of people who actually experienced the Great War first hand that I took a more intense interest. By then all my grandparents and other close friends or relatives of that era were dead.

In about 1985 I had the great pleasure of meeting a man in Kidderminster, a Mr. Moule I seem to recall, who had served on the Somme and with hindsight I can see that he wanted to tell me all about it. I deeply regret not telling him to turn off the cauliflower cheese he was making himself at the time and taking him out for a long lavish lunch at my expense. What good value that would have been! In the event I did what I had to do and then left him to his meagre and lonely repast. I know by default that he is no longer with us and one of the very few regrets I have in life is that missed opportunity.

The reason I know that my erstwhile acquaintance has died is that the last soldier from the trenches of the Great War died in 2009 and his name was Harry Patch. I read Harry's autobiography a while ago and, frankly, it is not that memorable. He served for a matter of months but has become famous for that rather than for any other aspect of a life which lasted over 110 years. Born in Somerset toward the end of Victoria's reign, he grew up during the Edwardian era and seems to have been a happy child of a relatively prosperous family. He tells of how he used chemicals to destroy nests of wasps and there is an unmistakable sense of irony that he was to become involved in the tail-end of a war that had seen the use of similar techniques on the men of both sides. His was a quarrying area but his house stood firmly and unaffected by tunnels directly beneath it. The yellow stone of that locality becomes much harder and turns grey when exposed to the air and I can imagine that some of those properties affect the indigenous population as if the secret is in the water. Whilst Harry could never be described as yellow, in the sense of cowardly, it is clear that he hardened with life and especially as he turned grey with age.

He had already started working for a living when notable events such as the sinking of the Titanic and the Suffragette movement were headline news. He was not a volunteer but reached prime fighting age by the time conscription came in and he was obliged to 'do his bit' with the Duke of Cornwall's Light Infantry. As a clever man he was soon given promotion to the rank of Lance Corporal. However, in a case of easy come easy go, some minor disciplinary offence resulted in demotion which was never re-gained. Nevertheless he was an expert marksman and was awarded a badge styled with crossed guns to show this although it was more important to Harry to be paid at a higher daily rate to reflect this skill.

His posting was as second man in a team which operated a Lewis gun and his specific role was to maintain and repair it when it jammed. He was soon wounded in the stomach and sent home to England to recover. At first he was in a convalescence home close to where I live now but was then sent to the Isle of Wight, a place I love and to where I have been a frequent visitor for many years. Armistice was declared before he went back into action and he became a time-served plumber in civvy street. Now, apart from fiddling about with pipery, true plumbers earn their living by working sheets of lead as flashings, roof coverings and ornamental architectural features.

During the course of one such engagement, the construction of what amounts to a tobacco-sponsored campanile in Bristol, he placed two new pennies beneath the lead covering to a trap door and presumably they are still there. On the same job, the tower was struck by lightning but Harry escaped unhurt. He has outlived a wife or two as well as his two sons, one of which shared the name Dennis with my father and the other of which shared the birth year of 1924 with my father. They were both embroiled in the Second World War but, as Harry was already in his forties when it broke out, his contribution was as a member of the Auxiliary Fire Service. My paternal grandfather, Harold, who was three years older than Harry, did the same.

In 2008, our then Poet Laureate, Andrew Motion, who incidentally shares a birth year with me, composed a piece in honour of Harry having become the last survivor of the trenches. As I understand it, that is what Poets Laureate are supposed to do so that is fair enough in principle. However, the outcome was very disappointing as a poem. It has a good first line, which was lifted directly from Harry's book, but it goes downhill from there on. It comprises five verses which bear a passing resemblance to sonnets, in that each has fourteen lines of ten syllables, but for me the connection with poetry ends there as each verse is a single sentence sprinkled with commas that do little to make it read more flowingly and there are few if any rhymes or any other poetic devices to help it along.

It is not for me to criticise the work of a Poet Laureate, although many do, but when Harry's 110th birthday came along in June 2008 I decided to write a poem for him and send it to him, as indeed I did. Inevitably the content of mine is not dissimilar to that of Andrew's, how could it be when we are both writing about the life of the same man? However, I chose to emphasise the fact that mine is a poem by writing it in rhyming couplets albeit with heavy use of enjambment. I am not a great admirer of this style of poetry either, as it reminds me of Rupert Bear stories from my childhood, but with the use of iambic pentameter wherever I could, I am reasonably satisfied with the result. At least it can be recognised as a poem even if not as a good poem.

See what you think as you read *'The Oldest Soldier'* which is not only a descriptive title but one which also echoes an earlier poem of mine, *'The Old Soldier'* which first appeared in *'Across my World'* and which, as you already know, was based upon an entirely different person whose path I crossed in 1967.

The Oldest Soldier

Oh, Harry Patch, how did you live so long
yet still maintain your sense of right and wrong?
A Victorian, born in Somerset,
your Edwardian childhood did not let
you forget or regret those pre-war years
when nests of wasps were the greatest of fears.
Potassium cyanide gassed them dead,
how could you see then where you would be led?

Tunnels from the quarry under your land
could not make it sink nor crumble like sand.
Although never yellow, like local stone,
you harden and turn grey but never moan.
A working lad were you when icebergs struck
a White Star liner that ran out of luck.
You also saw the Pankhursts chase the vote
for women, and for men of little note.

And so to war you never saw as yours
but called up to support your Country's cause.
Your lance-jack stripe was taken easily
but then for matters disciplinary
you lost it and your upper arm was bare
of decoration, but you didn't care.
The Duke of Cornwall's infantry so light
could never make you really want to fight.

The crossed guns badge you won put up your pay,
by sixpence more than the shilling per day.
You joined a Lewis team as number two
to clear the deadly pipework for your crew.
And you caught a packet – a Blighty one
of gut-tearing shrapnel sent by the Hun.
The Midlands first then Vectis, green and white,
saw you get well but not again to fight.

The war was over and you had a wife
so, Harry Patch, you led a normal life.
With peaceful pipework a living you earned
and sheets of five pound lead you teased and turned.
Two coppers bright you placed within a door
beneath the Great George bell on the top floor
of the Wills Tower in Bristol. Lightning struck
but missed you by another stroke - of luck.

In nineteen twenty you'd become a dad
and, four years later, sired another lad.
Your sons grew up and saw war of their own
in which you served again, but you had grown
too old to fight, except against the fires
caused by those German bombs on English Shires.
And then, at last, you had great age and fame,
when 'England's Final Tommy' was your name.

First published in shortened form in Reach Poetry Issue 136 January 2010

During the mid-1980s I was living in Sutton Coldfield which to me at that time was more or less a rural idyll. I had spent more than thirty years before moving there as a resident of the Black Country where the only birds we saw were sparrows and racing pigeons and the only animals we saw, apart from pets and rats, were safely locked away in Dudley Zoo.

My son, Andrew, has always been an early riser and even in his teenage years when most of his contemporaries had not only the ability but also the desire to sleep until lunchtime, he was not one to languish. However, that is not to say that he was hyper-active either: he would forsake his bed for the settee and spend as much time as he could watching television. During our Sutton Coldfield phase, he became a devoted, possibly obsessive, fan of the film *'The Great Escape'* and watched it in whole or in part on forty seven consecutive mornings before the rest of the house stirred.

Disturbing, but not distracting, him one day I drew back the curtains just in time to see two foxes slowly crossing our garden from right to left. The movement of the curtains attracted their attention but they did not change pace or break step. It probably took less than thirty seconds for them to complete their journey but it seemed longer and I was able to take in a great deal of detail of these, the first wild animals to enter my micro-world. One was larger than the other and eyed me seductively, in a way that told me it was female.

I had just about formulated the idea of reaching for my camera when the visit ended but the vision remains with me still despite the even more rural places in which I have lived since. Before a row of trees reached its current size I could see sheep and cows from the window of my study in Lichfield and in winter I still can. We also receive frequent visits from squirrels and we have counted up to twelve different varieties of birds in our garden on the same day so I feel I am at one with Nature in that respect. These comments are of course made from the viewpoint of a boy raised in West Bromwich!

Whilst domiciled in the nearly-rural part of Halesowen in the early 1990s, I had another early morning encounter with a fox. By then urban foxes were more commonplace and the Clent Hills were only just the other side of the A456 so this would not have come as a great surprise except that this one was clearly mad. I had reversed my car off the drive to go to work and, as I started to move forward, I saw this fox a few yards ahead frantically chasing her tail. I use the feminine pronoun because it may have been my erstwhile admirer having tracked me down over the miles and years since our brief encounter, but I don't really suppose it was!

Anyway, it was 8.30 a.m. and the spot she had chosen to put on her little show was directly outside the gates of a primary school at which small children were about to arrive. Convinced that the creature had taken leave of her senses, and reverting to my pre-Sutton Coldfield belief that wild animals were all just that, wild, I stopped the car and called the police on my recently acquired car phone as I had no wish to risk being savaged by getting out of the car to call from home. In truth, I had it in mind to keep the engine running and to use the car as either a weapon or as a barrier in the event that a child arrived before the seventh cavalry, or at least the local Plod.

To my astonishment, the desk sergeant was of no help at all and suggested that either I should arrest the animal myself or that I should call the RSPCA. During the heated exchange that followed, in which respective responsibilities for any injuries were made clear, as was the matter of who paid whose wages, the fox became bored and slinked away into someone else's back garden and I continued my journey in order that I may earn enough to contribute my share of the desk sergeant's wages. Perhaps that someone else was about to open the curtains, having stepped over a seven year old watching the VTR. If so, that child may have had his own great escape!

The sonnet *'Vixen'* deals mainly with the romantic aspects of my story, doesn't it?

Vixen

Oh, Foxy Lady in my garden caught
on film, or was it just in my mind's eye
that you and I were there without a thought
of being even closer by and by.
The curtains opened as you walked toward
the wooden fence, protective of your cub
who saw the gap left by the missing board
concealed from my sight by the flowering shrub.
Her copper crown and yours of varied hue
made vivid contrast with the parted bush
through which she passed, not wide enough for two.
The rustling leaves relieved the perfect hush
as, calmly, she then you slipped from my view
first her black-tipped nose, last your bronze-tipped brush.

First published as a prize-winning entry in Reach Poetry in April 2008. Issue 120

Since the early days of their fame, and especially since those wonderful days of 1963 about which I wrote *'Dear John'* in 2006, I have been enormously fond of The Beatles. My first written reference to them came in *'Summer of Love'* in 1967. By the time they disbanded in 1970 I had acquired more or less their complete recorded works on vinyl discs of different sizes and playing speeds. That was not easy as cash was in short supply throughout that time, but I did persuade a much better-heeled classmate to sell me some of the albums, or LPs as we called them in those days, at about half price as he became tired of them and moved onto something else. I suspect that he was being kind to me and that he went out and bought new replacements the day after each transaction. In the years that followed I was to use my own funds to replicate my collection on eight track stereo cartridges, cassette tapes and most recently on compact disc, with a few video tapes and DVDs thrown in for good measure.

One of the vinyl recordings that I bought new from John Turner's shop in Paradise Street, West Bromwich was *'Magical Mystery Tour'*. This was what was known as an EP which stood for 'extended player' and whilst being the size of 'a single' that is to say 7 inches in diameter, it contained several tracks on each side rather than just one each side like a single. In essence this was the soundtrack to the television film of the same name which I clearly remember being screened on BBC2 at 9.20 p.m. on Boxing Day 1967. I was at my paternal grandparents' house at that time but managed to watch it in black and white on something like a 15 inch screen. I thought it was great but it was slammed by the critics and didn't receive true acclaim for many years.

For my birthday in 2007, Denise, booked us on a trip to Liverpool to enjoy the various museum-style tributes to the lads and we stayed overnight in the Adelphi Hotel. The following poem needs no further explanation for those who know the music, each verse is inspired by a song or instrumental track from the film. If you don't know it, buy it now and enjoy!

Magical Mystery Tour

She took the invitation
and made a reservation
to start the celebration
of my fifty sixth year

'We'll be there quite soon' she said
'I have booked a room and bed,
wine and songs can fill your head
Happy Birthday, Graham dear'

Now we're flying to the dock
in a race against the clock
with a circuit of the block
till we came to Albert's pier

Then we joined the tail-end row
of the queue to see the show
but my Mom should always know
when the front was getting near

And then just ahead of us
were the kids from the school 'bus
with their leader, Sir Walrus
who once lived not far from here

But our faces grew not long
like the girl in the old song
or the boy, I may be wrong
it was all a little queer

Thousand voices spoke out loud
as the World span from the crowd.
The eyes in my head, though bowed,
shed many a wistful tear

Now that half of them have gone
and the others soldier on
without Harrison or John,
Jules and Dhani have our ear

176

Devon has always been a favourite holiday destination for me. From the middle 1970s when the extended M5 and a more reliable car (fuelled by company petrol) allowed me to venture further from home than Weston Super Mare, the Torbay area was first choice until Denise and I had a fleeting preference for the north coast in the early years of the new millennium before settling on the delightful town of Dartmouth.

We have since spent several holidays in rented houses overlooking the river with the Naval College to the left of the picture and the castle to the right. The largely residential town of Kingswear is directly opposite us and this is at least as easy on the eye when lit up at night as it is during the day when it takes the direct sunlight while Dartmouth is in shadow. Obviously, such beauty inspired me to write a poem about it a while ago and this follows. The meanings are very clear in the main and do not really require any further explanation. However, for any readers who may not have a particular interest in engineering and/or history, it might be useful to mention that Thomas Newcomen was born in the town in 1663 and that he went on to develop one of the first successful steam engines. Hearing a modern car straining to climb the hill named after one of Dartmouth's most famous sons one day, I felt a sense of irony and I also wondered if Mr. Newcomen ever had the slightest inkling that one day a type of engine would be made that was so small, mobile and powerful as to be capable of moving a ton of metal up the very steep slopes of his home town.

One man who certainly did have visions of the future was Isambard Kingdom Brunel. Unfortunately his foresight was not so good as to see that he would not be allowed to run his new train line over a bridge into Dartmouth. He had already built the station to receive it and so had to build another on Kingswear side which to this day runs a steam train to and from Paignton. The original building remains on the river's edge and is home to a restaurant and to the purveyors of splendid fish and chips that I do my very best to resist but usually with little success.

This is **'Dartmouth'**.

Dartmouth

To see the green-clad mounds rise from the Dart
and take on colours, like an artist's board,
is easy on the eye – to say the least.
A cedar tree stands proud upon a ridge
on Kingswear side. The castle and the fort,
past sandstone cliffs, stand to the South and East.

I hear the sounds of daily river life
with wind and diesel giving gentle power
to yachts and ferries, plying bank to bank.
And then the straining engine of a Ford,
in lowest gear to climb Newcomen's hill,
drowns out the squawk of seagulls with its clank.

The feel of granite steps beneath my feet,
as I work hard to walk up Crowthers Hill,
then yields to shallow mud in Dyers Wood.
And rugged stone which forms the Castle walls
is matched in hardness by the iron guns
and shot, for defence only - as they should.

A briney breeze leaves salt upon my lips
which seasons local crab upon my plate
and not-so-local cod with chips, fresh-fried.
A Saint Emilion goes well with both
despite its colour. Never criticise
drinking red wine with fish until you've tried.

My nostrils sense the seaweed in the creek.
Some say 'the smell of ozone' but they're wrong
as, odourless, that gas has no place here.
And on the wind a sulphur-laden cloud,
of water vapour, wafts across the Dart
as Brunel's dream steams back into Kingswear.

First published in The Dawntreader. December 2009

178

I'm not altogether sure where the initial idea came from but, as a surprise present for my birthday in July 2008, Denise bought me a short holiday in Bruges. Presumably from the same source emerged the idea that I should buy her a similar holiday, but not as a surprise, for her birthday in September and that we should take our presents at the same time. We therefore made plans to travel by Eurostar one Sunday in mid-September and arrangements were made to take a taxi to Birmingham as the earliest train to leave Lichfield was too late for the latest train to take us from Birmingham to Euston from where we had to walk to St Pancras for the connection.

A day or two before we were due to travel, a truck caught fire in the Channel Tunnel and services through it were suspended. After a great deal of re-organisation, we took the taxi to Derby instead and caught a connection directly to St. Pancras where we met our travel guide by the John Betjeman statue and took a motor coach on to Dover where we became foot passengers on the ferry to Calais. There was a bomb scare at Calais which kept us and our luggage apart for a while until we boarded another motor coach as the fifth and final leg of a thirteen hour journey to Bruges.

In the period between my birthday and our departure we had spoken to several friends who had visited Bruges and they were unanimous in saying what a beautiful but very expensive place it is. For the first day or so that we were there it failed to come up to that high expectation but we soon warmed to it and had a very pleasant few days during which we also took part in an excursion to Tyne Cot Cemetery, Hill 62, and the amazing town of Ypres. Bruges itself seemed to me to be beautiful, peaceful but vibrant and, above all, enchanting.

However, it became clear from the comments made by our guide on a walking tour of the town that the antiquity of it all was largely a myth. A particular bridge over the canal, described as being medieval in all the literature, was actually less than two hundred years old as were the pretty gabled frontages of the shops and restaurants facing the Market Square.

As far as I could make out, there was one wall that had a reasonable claim to having been built a few centuries ago and everything else was either a replacement for something of similar vintage or simply something built to look old.

Our hotel was immediately adjacent to a bell tower which had a winding staircase of 366 steps from court yard level to the top gallery but I was more interested in the fact that the tower leans significantly away from the vertical and was clearly built at different times and in badly clashing architectural styles.

Belgium in general is renowned for its beer and its chocolate and so tours of both a brewery and of a small chocolate factory were essential. The brewery trip and its sample of two types of beer, resulted in Denise acquiring a taste for the lighter brew, which is freely available in Waitrose, but little could be seen and less learned about brewing as, like in all other modern breweries, it comprises a series of metal tanks connected to each other by sealed pipery.

The image I had of a be-whiskered, red- faced old gentleman in an white apron stirring the brew in a bubbling open vat with a long wooden spoon was shattered, I may as well have travelled for fifteen minutes from home and toured the clinical Coors brewery in Burton on Trent.

The chocolate factory, the rear room behind a shop in truth, was interesting and impressive but again not entirely free of disillusionment as we were informed that they actually buy the chocolate in big slabs which are melted down and altered in various ways before the sweet brown liquid is poured into moulds to form the end products which are then sold in the shop, and very delicious they are too!

Perhaps because we had also been programmed to expect everything to cost a fortune, we were pleasantly surprised to discover that this is not the case provided that the warnings of the tour guides are heeded and that certain restaurants and bars which face the main square are avoided. The same is of course true of most towns and cities.

As I hinted at above, Bruges rose above all of these observations and became as charming to us as it had to our friends. I remain unsure as the how much truth there is in some other stories that abound, such as the promise to look after the town's swans in perpetuity as payment for some favour granted to the town by a Monarch many years ago. Just off the main square, there are many excellent restaurants and bars that serve good food at a reasonable price; we ate Flemish stew in one of them one evening and, because we enjoyed it so much, we had exactly the same the following evening although we did chose another restaurant.

180

The menu outside another proudly boasted of its belly pork with herbs which was quite amusing as we had misheard our guide when she gave its name as La Belle Époque.

Another feature that Bruges shares with other cities, including Amsterdam which we were to visit a month later, is the use by its inhabitants of bicycles. In other places, including on the path along the River Thames near to Richmond, I have found cyclists to be most disrespectful to pedestrians and to deliver angry glances or even comments if they are forced to stop or change direction to avoid a walker who was unaware of the approaching terror on two wheels. This was not the case with the good citizens of Bruges who seemed to me to take great care not to inconvenience pedestrians by their massive presence on every street and in every square.

One morning we stumbled upon a battalion of Grenadier Guards in the Market Square and this instantly brought back to mind the thoughts of Ypres and of earlier visits by the British army to those parts. However, this time the soldiers comprised a marching band which was welcomed equally by the tourists and by the locals who clearly still feel some affection towards us as a nation, certain by comparison to some of our other European neighbours. I have no idea what the band was doing there but it was good to see.

The next poem simply commemorates that holiday with a great deal of fondness although I do make a nod of acknowledgement to the style of Sylvia Plath in verse six.

I offer it to you under the less-than imaginative name of *'Bruges'*.

Bruges

Your brilliance, like moonlight, is a lie;
reflected glory from a burning ball
of gas makes lunar luminosity
and yours comes from your medieval wall.

Your bell-tower with its leap-year steps
is ill-designed and tilting to the side
as tourist rivers flow to sup from cups
in Square-side cafés, warned of by the guide.

Your crow-step gables and government block
are nowhere near as old as we were told,
nor are the bridges that straddle the creek
worn and torn by years and years that have rolled.

Your brewery has no visible vat,
just stainless steel tanks and tubes, like the rest,
and chocolate, well enough of all that,
it is made elsewhere and moulded at best.

and yet………………..

and yet..........................

Your magical charm wins over the best
of the brains and the footfall that follows
cerebral satisfaction, with the nests
of swans and cygnets weeping with willows.

Your restaurants and cafés are superb
with their Flemish stew and their Flemish stew,
more belle époque than belly pork with herbs,
and beers, blonde and dark, more than a few.

Your cyclists, who inhabit every street
and pedal on where walkers wander free,
accept that bicycles came after feet
and swerve around the tourists happily.

Your Square again plays host as soldiers brave,
but marching now with bugles not big guns,
complete the symbiotic tie we crave,
the mutual respect that runs and runs.

First published in Reach Poetry October 2009 Issue 133

From time to time, the wish to return my body to something approaching the shape it used to be prompts me to join one or other of the various health clubs that we have here in Lichfield. The usual pattern is that, for a month or two, I attend every few days for the mind-numbing exercise of running, walking or cycling for an hour without getting anywhere, followed by a swim, a sauna or both. Most recently this activity has been taking place at what used to be Seedy Mill Golf Club but which has been expensively upgraded to include all manner of facilities including a half-decent restaurant. An English breakfast after a few lengths of the pool can make a Sunday morning quite a pleasure but since my health scare such gastronomic pleasures have been forsaken.

On one occasion Denise and I were in the pool when a young blonde girl came in and went up and down effortlessly, doing three lengths to my one without the need to stop for a breather at each end. The three of us then moved on to the jacuzzi where we lay in the warm, foaming water for about fifteen minutes to ease the muscles. It was while we lay there that I noted the troubled look on the girl's face. I had judged her to be of Polish or similar extraction, not unlike the tall blonde athletes that make tennis almost worth watching these days. In those few minutes I explained to myself the worried look on her face despite all the obvious attributes she had in terms of looks, fitness and youth, by deciding that she had a family at home which lived in very different circumstances to hers and by raising the possibility that she may at some stage be compelled to return to that sort of life. Probably utter nonsense but it occupied my mind for a while.

I also noted that the serene English beauty of Denise's face did not fully conceal a sadness behind the eyes and I was reminded of her own health and other concerns for the future. It occurred to me that the agitated water of the jacuzzi is at odds with the restful effect that lying in it has and that, to the same extent, the sadness behind the eyes is at odds with the good looks and seemingly luxurious lives of those two beautiful girls. So, of course, I wrote another sonnet about it and here it is.

I call it 'Turbulence' with allusion to the waters of the jacuzzi as well as to the minds of two lovely ladies.

184

Turbulence

The boiling pool of turbulent anger
belies the calming of a peaceful spa.
Likewise, a fair face from Eastern Europe
shows worry and concern for those afar.
Her sculptured body eased through twenty lengths
to six of mine, we stroked in even time.
In the tub my visage was the calmer
as fears for later life invade her prime.

By my side there is a greater beauty
whose hopes and happiness are sometimes marred
by illness and life's sick sense of humour
which make her feel she should be on her guard.

For the first girl hope comes from up above
but, for my wife, strength will come from my love.

Since the early 1960s and the success of Gerry Marsden's song *'Ferry cross the Mersey'*, I had a low-priority item on my to-do list which involved availing myself of that particular form of transport. Until about 2002 my many crossings of the Mersey had all involved tunnels but during a weekend stay with our friends, John and Jean Bacon of Gateacre, we decided to take a trip on the ferry. Leaving John's car outside the Liver Building, for which he later incurred a parking fine, we went aboard. As we waited to cast off, I saw an object on the surface of the water which caught my eye. It was bluey-purple and white in colour and appeared to be entirely unaffected by the current of the river, by the wind, by the rise and fall of the ferry with the swell or, indeed, by anything. Other matter such as leaves, lollipop sticks and cigarette cartons came by but the bluey-purple and white article stayed exactly where it was.

My mind, conversely, started to wander. As far as I could judge, it was a few inches in length and the colours started me thinking of my football club, West Bromwich Albion, which does not have a particularly good record against Liverpool FC. Perhaps the article was part of a scarf thrown into the river by an angry Albion fan after yet another defeat.

Then I remembered that there is a second football club in Liverpool and that they, Everton FC, also play in blue and white and have little more success against the Reds than my club does. So perhaps the erstwhile owner of the article was a local chap.

Then it came to me, in 1917 the poet Sigfried Sassoon threw the ribbon of the Military Cross he had won for bravery in action against the Germans into the Mersey. His actions were so brave that he earned the nickname 'Mad Jack' but he had become disenchanted with the war and had started to protest against it. The throwing away of his medal ribbon was part of this protest but perhaps the Mersey had held it for him to reclaim one day from the same spot.

In truth, what I saw was the wrapper from a bar of Cadbury's chocolate but I did enjoy my five minute reverie and it inspired my next poem which I called *'The Ribbon'*.

The Ribbon

I saw a ribbon, blue and white,
just floating by the ferry.
It drifted neither left nor right
nor did its stream-flow vary.
It seemed that, for a hundred years,
that rag had been unmoving.
Its spot was set, just past the piers,
in silent swell, so soothing.

At first I thought, quite naturally,
that it was just another
scarf abandoned, frustratedly
by a footballing brother.
From Hawthorns or from Goodison,
the defeats are much the same,
when faced with Anfield's champions,
the Masters of that great game.

But then I saw the rag was small,
much smaller than a scarf is.
So what was it, how did it fall
onto the Mersey's surface?
Or was it thrown, in Mad Jack's rage,
in protest at the slaughter?
His words preserved upon the page,
his ribbon on the water.

A high proportion of my poems is about people. In the main they are in praise of the subject, Gordon Brown and his odious henchmen being the most frequent exceptions. Perhaps my recent break from writing is in part because Gordon has gone to ground following his 2010 Election humiliation and I am not as yet angry enough with anyone to replace him as a whipping boy. Several union leaders who need putting in their places are strong contenders.

It is not often that the opportunity to pay tribute to two people arises within one poem, especially when those people never met and were half a generation apart in age and when one of them has been dead for well over forty years. I have been aware of the existence of a poet by the name of Sylvia Plath, already fondly referred to in *'Bruges'*, for as long as I can remember but I only read a small sample of her work many years ago before dismissing her and her poetry as being thoroughly depressing. Perhaps I pre-judged the situation as a result of my having known that she did in fact take her own life at an early age. To be perfectly honest, she has often been confused with Iris Murdoch in my mind although I am not entirely sure why that should be as they didn't really have that much in common with each other. Within the past four or five years a series of events has taken place to draw my attention to Sylvia Plath for the first time in decades, including a feature film about her life and a recent interest in her shown by Denise.

In turn, Denise is a great admirer of the singer and songwriter Ralph McTell who wrote a song about Sylvia Plath over thirty years ago but with which I have only become familiar in recent years since seeing Ralph in concert in Lichfield where he played it. It is therefore Sylvia Plath who is the principal subject of the poem which follows although I also pay tribute to Ralph within it. Without this explanation you may have thought that I was referring to one of my several ancestors of that name, mentioned elsewhere. Ralph, that is, although I did have one relative called Sylvia too.

One of Sylvia's best known poems is called *'Tulips'* and in Ralph's song he admits to an admiration of Sylvia and attributes this to 'the one about the tulips'.

For my part, I think it was the one called *'Daddy'* that did it. You will be aware from earlier in this book that my own father died in late 2007 and when I was reminded that Sylvia Plath, whose father died when she was a child, had a poem of that title, I read it and managed to listen online to a recording of her reading it.

I suppose I was expecting, and I was certainly hoping, that she would have words to which I could relate as I grieved for Dad.

As it happens *'Daddy'* is nothing like the type of poem that I was expecting but nevertheless I found it a fascinating piece of work and to hear it read by Sylvia herself was magical. No-one can make the 'ooo' sound quite like she did and *'Daddy'* has lots of line-end and internal rhymes with that sound. I also listened to her reading 'Tulips' but as there was no such thing as 'online' when Ralph became a fan, he must have used his own exceptional talent to read it properly for himself.

'Tulips' is about Sylvia being in hospital and she was clearly upset by a dozen red tulips that, I assume, were bought for her by her husband, the then future Poet Laureate Ted Hughes.

Now, Sylvia also published a book. Called *'The Bell Jar'*, it is more or less an autobiography and was brilliantly written and bears testimony to the fact that the World lost a great deal when Sylvia died with so little written and even less published. The leading character in the book stands five feet ten inches tall in stockinged feet and she very clearly has an aversion to shorter men. My theory is that one of the main reasons why she pursued Ted Hughes to the point of marriage and beyond was the fact that he was six foot or more in height although I would readily accept that she may have liked his poems too, unlike me I must add.

I also think that she saw him as a replacement for her father. Sadly, he took control of her writings after her death and failed to publish as much as he could have. Indeed he went so far as to change what she herself had intended to publish. I first called my poem *'Sylvia'* but I then changed it very slightly to distinguish it from the title of Ralph's song.

For Sylvia

Did Daddy do it?
I don't know if that was the case or not.
Was it the book?
I don't think so but perhaps I just forgot.

For Ralph it was the bright red blooms
that led him to write those words.
Their colour shone forth from your gloom
and sang like a dozen birds.
I tried and tried, I thought and thought
but never could quite see why
the glimpse of brightness that he brought
should so much offend your eye.
I heard that from your very tongue
and then Daddy too, one day.
My own had gone, not very long,
I wondered what you would say.

By then I had you like a drug
and I could not put you down.
Your writing bit me like a bug
but every line wore a frown.

I think your Daddy rose again
in a body chosen for height.
I know this one suppressed your pen
after you left us that night.

First published in Reach Poetry February 2010. Issue 138

190

There are some poems which need absolutely no introduction whatsoever. Both the subject and content of them is so obvious that further explanation would add nothing. *'Nuptials'* is one such poem. While the subject matter of it is of the utmost importance, it is difficult to add to what is very obvious; it is about my son's wedding.

'Echoes' is another but for a different reason. Whilst the first could only have been inspired by my son's wedding, the second could have been inspired by any one of several things. I believe that its meaning is clear but perhaps not. Indeed, in its original form, which was entitled *'Fading'*, it conveyed a sad, dismal feeling that was never intended. The message is clear and simple that you can enjoy the touch of a loved one over and over again, fuelled by memory, but that it is much better to have it renewed every now and then for the rest of one's life.

'Fading' seemed to imply that the life in question was nearing its end and that just one more touch should be enough to last until then. I hope that the re-write successfully converts a sad poem to a happy one. Both set out to bring together the two senses of hearing and touch and the emotion of love into one short verse.

'Lundy' was inspired by a weekend spent in 2008 looking at the island of that name from the seaside town of Woolacombe. In 1988 we had a short holiday there during which Andrew and Catherine insisted on swimming in an outside pool at the Woolacombe Bay Hotel despite the fact that they practically had to break the ice on the surface to get in. This was made all the more remarkable by the fact that a few short months previously, Catherine had been hospitalised with pneumonia. That is probably the first time that she, if not her brother too, will recall staying in a decent hotel as holidays in the earlier years of their lives were usually spent in a caravan. Every evening I thought of Pavlov's dog as the restaurant bell was sounded to let us know that dinner was served. The 2008 visit was brought about by an invitation that Denise and I had received from Jamie Rawsthorn. Jamie is the son of one of my oldest friends, Robert, and his dear wife Angela with whom we have spent countless weekends and summer holidays at their home on the Isle of Wight. Both *'Monuments'* and *'The Angel and the Snake'* were inspired by one of those visits.

But again I digress. I have known Jamie all his life, as well as his little sister Elizabeth to whom I have always regarded myself as a secular godfather. Jamie now stands very nearly two metres in height and is a serving police officer following in the rather large footsteps of his late grandfather. He also has a lovely wife, Tess, and it was their decision to marry that led to the trip to Woolacombe. They had decided to spend a year touring the World and to marry at some point en route but, as they didn't want to deprive their friends and relations of the opportunity to share the celebrations, they held the wedding reception before they went. They are both keen surfers and Woolacombe is one of their favourite haunts so the choice of venue was easy.

Of course I knew of Lundy Island, as a fairly regular visitor to the North Devon coast myself, but I nevertheless associate it more with the BBC Radio shipping forecasts. For the record, I am also aware that officially the area is just *'Lundy'*, that another area is just *'Portland'* and that *'Finisterre'* has been re-named *'FitzRoy'*. But this is a book of poems, not an encyclopaedia so if you want facts look elsewhere!

What did intrigue me was that the island seemed to move in and out of the bay according to the precise spot from which I observed it. I have a trained eye for size and distance but I couldn't ignore this particular illusion. If this were to be an encyclopaedia it would also be able to explain why I could also see the Moon over the island despite the bright October sunshine.

Actually I do know why that is but that doesn't stop me being fascinated whenever I see it.

Nuptials

So now, my son, you've come to take a wife,
someone to love and cherish from the heart.
A haven too, against the storms of life
when we have gone, who loved you from the start.
For nearly thirty years you've graced my door
with gladness, sometimes sadness, and with pride
and now, my son, you've come to bring yet more
joy as I welcome in your lovely bride.

You two are one, or so that cliché runs
but neither one was less than whole till now,
as each of you could fill up tuns and tuns
with sports and schools success before this vow.
With symbiotic strength you'll go great guns
we're very proud of you, so take a bow.

Echoes

Your tender touch starts tactile echoes
that I can feel
after the touch has gone.
Like all echoes,
each is fainter than the one before.
They never end,
they just get softer.
To a point at which they are no longer heard.
Or felt.
Touch me again, as you once did.
And then again
to keep the echoes coming.
Until I can feel no more.

First published in Reach Poetry. June 2010. Issue number 141

Lundy

A radio star like Finisterre,
or German Bight or Portland Bill,
now you are here and now you are there,
seeming much closer from the hill.
Behind you I see the day-time Moon,
in brightest sunshine from the side,
your terns provide a feathered festoon
as you float on the ebbing tide.

The Red Barn stands firm upon the bend,
a few yards from the Bay Hotel
where my children swam with health to mend,
an icy dip before the bell.
Another child has grown up, and how,
and leaves the beat and takes a wife.
They journey around the World for now
before they start their married life.

I sincerely hope that my cousin, Maureen, will forgive me for mentioning the fact that she is a few years older than me although, like her mother and grandmother before her, she is wearing very well indeed! She has been an enormous influence on me since I was born and she and her husband, Steve, remain frequent companions to Denise and I during visits to restaurants, theatres and European cities.

It was during one such visit, Amsterdam to be precise, that it became clear to me that the painful leg that had caused her so much trouble in recent times had worsened to the point at which something simply had to be done about it. She was suffering far more than I was despite my eighteen seasons of being felled by oafish full backs every week on the parks and playing fields around West Bromwich.

Sure enough, she arranged to have a replacement joint which has helped a great deal in restoring her mobility but until a fairly late stage before the operation was decided upon she had been more inclined to the view that one of her hip joints was the main source of her discomfort. The X-rays told a different tale and they seem to have been right.

I decided that the occasion needed a poem but that it should take the form of an ode to the knee from Maureen.

I therefore wrote the poem that follows as a sort of amanuensis for her but, other than to explain that Maureen married Steve at a church dedicated to Saint Mary, it needs no other clarification as it is light and simple and intended purely or fun.

The Knee

O wondrous joint you served me well
for six decades of toil and strife,
you caught me when I tripped and fell
and turned your skin to rarest beef.

Then later, as I make my vow
at Saint Mary's I genuflect
with so much ease I wonder now,
why did I not give you respect?

I thought your ball and socket mate
had done her best but brought me pain,
until the Roentgen rays of late
showed me you were the one to blame.

So now we end our life-long tryst
as I put plastic in your place
and metal too, now there's the twist -
I'll leave you now to rust in peace.

By 1968 I was just about old enough to sign up for the Army, had I been so inclined, but I didn't for the simple reason that by then I was firmly committed to the 'make love, not war' ethos that was prevalent among the youth of that decade. I had missed the chance to take part in the Great War by at least half a century. Nevertheless, I have always been fiercely proud of my English heritage and I have often wondered how I could make some tangible contribution to the protection of it without resorting to shooting or dropping bombs on anyone, despite the repeated disputes with Germany on the football field that we continue to have.

My paternal grandfather was confined to munitions work during the Great War and, as previously mentioned, I have exemption papers that he carried with him at that time. In the Second World War, he was too old to fight but joined the Auxiliary Fire Service, as did the famous Harry Patch.

My father also found himself in a reserved occupation, as an electrical fitter, but spent his evenings carrying messages from one place to another, sometimes during air raids. Setting aside the pacifist traits that I still have, I also like my comfort and I cannot begin to imagine how I would have been able to endure trench life although it may have been only marginally worse for me than the noise and filth of a factory.

As far as football goes, I was never very good at keeping my nerve in front of goal, especially when taking penalties when I was young enough to play the game and, by the time I was able to stay calm through most things, I was too old to play football.

It had occurred to me that my part in any future war might be in some sort of Intelligence and Planning Corps with a Susannah York look-alike bringing me cups of tea every now and then. One day I saw a photograph for sale on e bay of a 1916 vintage soldier holding a clarinet. By then I had been playing clarinet for many years but the sight of the soldier reminded me of an old schoolmate, Chris Allen, who left us behind in the A level class in 1968 to join the Army as a musician.

A poem soon followed and the title, *'The Musical Soldier'* is with both him and the unknown warrior of the picture in mind.

The Musical Soldier

I missed the fight by fifty years or more
but always thought that I should do my bit
against the foe of nineteen sixty six
and other years since and some before.
My granddad made the bullets for the Somme
and put out fires started by the Blitz
whilst Father wired electrical bits
and, in the evening, dodged from bomb to bomb.

There never was a chance that I could live
within a trench with lice and rats and shells
but neither was the factory life for me,
with grease and grime and noise and sickly smells.
In any case, I never saw the point
of slaying cousins just because they may
decide to live on someone else's land
whilst ours was ours, unchallenged in those days.

I never could have scored the crucial goal
to make it 'now all over, four beats two',
my nerves at spot-kick time would also fail
and when the tide turned I was older too.
So there was my dilemma. How could I
protect my safety and my flesh and bone
and also hold my head up, feather-free
but always keep this England for her own?

I sometimes thought my answer lay with codes
or maps with markers in a room below
the streets of London, sheltered from the blast
of German bombs in that infernal home.
But forty years ago I knew a lad
who left the schoolroom we had shared for years
to join the Army, not to fire a gun
and not to bayonet a foreign chest.
He was a bandsman with a clarinet
who played his part to keep up the morale
and entertain the troops out on a march
but still remain a soldier through and through.

At last I saw a picture on e bay
of a squaddie with a clarinet
and all at once my visions hit the net,
an instrument that I can also play!
So there we have it. In another call
I'd trade Lee Enfield for Boosey and Hawkes
and hope for conciliatory talks
but still I'd catch the wounded as they fall.

Although I have been fortunate enough to drive rather nice cars for many years, I rarely derive the same amount of pleasure from driving them that I did in the days when my cars were less luxuriant by far but when the roads were less crowded; there are approximately four times the number of cars on England's roads today than there were when I started driving little more than forty years ago. In addition, we now have those infuriating speed cameras with huge fines for breaking some arbitrary speed limit, potential deprivation of the Human Right to drive if you get caught too often and a whole lot of people from various categories that shouldn't be allowed anywhere near a steering wheel.

For these reasons I sometimes take advantage of the two mainline stations that we have in Lichfield and catch a train. On one such occasion I was bound for a lunch in Manchester, changing at Stoke on Trent, and waited a few minutes at Trent Valley station for my train to arrive. In that short period of time several Virgin expresses went through at well over 100mph, leaning into the bends with an almost human quality, until mine arrived.

I never tire of seeing the three spires of Lichfield Cathedral from any angle, and that includes from a passing train but, in a strange way that can only be appreciated by those of us with an interest in civil engineering, the cooling towers of Rugeley Power Station also have a certain charm as they rise to meet the cloud cover over the undulating landscape. It has always fascinated me to think that the wall thickness of a cooling tower, relative to its height, in less than the shell of an egg.

For the next few miles the scene changes continuously and is beautiful in all ways until the blot on the landscape that is the Potteries approaches. Natural beauty harmonises with more miracles of construction such as canals and arched bridges built in local stone using traditional methods. Retaining walls comprising chunks of the same stone but contained in wire baskets to make huge building blocks, which are called gabions, combine sound structural engineering principles with Nature's bounty to complete the picture.

'Trent Valley Trip' takes us from the station of that name to the smoke of Stoke, which could be regarded as the Gateway to the North, with apologies to Peter Sellers and of course Balham!

Trent Valley Trip

Three spires proudly pierce a heavy sky
as tilting virgins pass by, fast and loose,
until the right one stops for me to mount
and ride towards my lunch-time rendezvous.

Then swollen watercourses slowly stroke
the lower pastures, with their banks unclear
and under stone-arched bridges, so divine,
with springers and with voussoirs on their piers.

The man-made waterways are no less full
with wonder, as with water, with their locks
to cross the hills to meadows, low and flat,
retained by gabions of broken rocks.

At every mile a spire or a tower,
all smaller than the three and those that poke
through misty hills, bejewelled by full-fleeced sheep.
How pleasant is my valley, south of Stoke

In *'Across my World'*, I included several poems written about various places I had visited over the years and, to a certain extent, I continued in the same vein in *'Out of the Shadow'* although those were mainly concerned with my favourite parts of England or the near European mainland. The exception is the one which follows which was inspired by a fabulous experience I had in April and May 2009.

Denise and I went via Dubai to Sydney where we were able to spend some time with Clare, Pete and Rebecca, shortly after Clare had discovered that she was to produce the baby boy which we now know as Ben. We were also able to meet up with a few schoolfriends, for the first time in some cases having thereto made and developed the friendship through the internet only. Others just happened to be in Sydney at the same time, living a few miles away from us at home, and one of which I last saw in the early 1970s.

We all had lunch together in the open air close to the Harbour Bridge and, appropriately for us 'ex pats', on St. George's Day.

A few days later was Anzac Day and I could not resist the temptation to play a small part in what I assumed would be a diluted version of our Remembrance Day. I could hardly have been more wrong! What happened was indeed like Remembrance Day but with Christmas Day, May Day, New Year's Eve and a Royal Wedding all rolled into one. The local folk know how to celebrate and to display respect for servicemen, dead or alive, at the same time. They all wear military medals if they have them, or on behalf of fallen relatives if they don't, and the centre of Sydney from the Rocks to the far side of Hyde Park is the site of a twenty hour party.

In a constant way, the Anzacs are also commemorated by a relatively new cable stay bridge which spans Johnston's Bay from Pyrmont to Glebe Island. It carries the flags of both Australia and New Zealand on its respective east and west pylons. It is visible for miles around and would be even more impressive if it were not for its iconic older relative nearby.

Having been familiar with the Harbour Bridge since I saw a photograph of it in a geography text book at school in the 1950s, I had subsequently learned that it had been built to the design of Sir Ralph Freeman a one–time senior partner of Freeman Fox and Partners, a well-known firm of Consulting Engineers. At least that is the English version of history.

It is certain that Freeman played a massive role in the project, as did the equally well known English firm of Dorman Long, the steelwork contractors, but in Australia there is far more emphasis on a chap called John Bradfield who I had previously half-recalled as having happened to have been no more than what we may call the Borough Surveyor at the time the bridge was built. It transpires that Bradfield actually spent decades nursing the project more or less from inception to completion, having personally chosen the design from several contenders, first in type and then in detail. The highway that the bridge carries is named in Bradfield's honour but Ralph Freeman does get a small mention on a plaque fixed to one of its parapet walls.

At first sight of the bridge 'in the flesh' I was underwhelmed as it seemed to me to be much heavier than necessary and it did not dominate the skyline in the same way as it did in my mind's eye from the 1950s photograph.

However, one day Denise and I were able to climb its arch to the summit, cross the crown to the other arch and down the other side. Through that experience we were able to appreciate the true scale of the thing and realise that it is still one of the highest two or three structures in Sydney. We were looking down at a steep angle upon the buildings that were the tallest prior to the bridge being built – the ones that I recalled from that old picture of my schooldays. The descent gave me another good view of Anzac Bridge as I drank an imaginary toast to those whose name it carries with pride.

The inevitable poem is, obviously I think, inspired in form by Wordsworth's scribblings on another bridge, Westminster to be precise, and you must therefore blame him not me for the fact that it is another sonnet. I have even used the same style as him for a very descriptive title although, probably like him, I didn't actually write it on the bridge. I wrote it back at Clare and Pete's house later the same day although I did have the first four lines in my head before I left the bridge.

Composed on Sydney Harbour Bridge. 24th April 2009

The Anzac Bridge is proud and cable stayed
and stands to honour those who joined the band
to battle for their mighty Motherland,
acknowledging the massive price they paid.
Gallipoli had served to raise the bar
for Aussie lads to match in other ways
and so they did, on many later days,
in evil, bloody conflicts near and far.

Now as I scale the awesome Harbour Bridge
and see its sturdy structure finely arched,
I strive to climb upon its rounded ridge
with aching legs and throat becoming parched
but not too dry to pay a fond homage
to all the Sydney heroes who have marched.

First published in Crab Lines off the Pier. Summer 2010

In 1963 I had the pleasure and privilege of befriending Andrew Robert Wharton as we both became pupils at West Bromwich Grammar School. The friendship continued, unbroken, until his untimely death on 7th July 2009 and I was given the additional privilege of acting as a pall bearer alongside his son, Matthew, at the funeral nine days later. We were backed up by four sturdy chaps who were former colleagues of Andy during his service with the police.

In our teens, Andy and I socialised in the ways that teens did then and on one occasion we attended the 1968 Christmas Party of the Black Country Society wearing Victorian costume and in the company of several other school friends. A photograph, which appeared in the local press, was taken and, many years later, I posted it on a couple of social networking websites, describing my dear, thin-faced friend, as 'cadaverous'. Andy was an accomplished pianist and provided much of the entertainment that evening, with the hit song of the day, 'Lily the Pink' being played many times. Only a few days before he died I was shown some of the photographs that later appeared in a book by local historian and author, Terry Price, and that same picture is one of them. For a couple of years in the late 1960s Andy also gave me piano lessons but I could never co-ordinate my right hand with my left so I eventually gave up trying. Instead, he taught me to drive a car, sitting patiently in the passenger seat of my 1959 Austin A35 for mile after mile around the Midlands and on several trips to Weston Super Mare. At about that time, we also became part of a group of old school friends which spanned several yearly cohorts and included several contemporaries of Andy's older brother, Roger. In mock public school style, Andy became known as **'Wharton Minor'** and hence the title of the next poem. Years later, when the group was re-formed and widened immensely, many more members of the Wharton family, all older than Andy, joined in so for a while I called him 'Wharton Minimus'. On one occasion he was on a course of anti-biotics and had been advised not to drink alcohol so he offered to drive a few of us on an evening out so then I called him 'Wharton Minibus'.

In 1974 I was given the honour of acting as Best Man at Andy's wedding to Ann Pinchin. He was working in Teignmouth at the time and a group of us had spent a long evening with him there on a stag night. Part of that was in a club with a singer called Lofty who rendered Elvis Presley's **'The Wonder of You'** more than once as our group provided the backing vocals. That song had become a favourite of Andy and I as it hit the top of the charts four years earlier, during one of our many holidays in Weston Super Mare and, on the rare occasions these days that I perform karaoke in public, that is the song I

206

sing. Somehow I don't think I shall be able to sing it again as I never could without remembering that night in Teignmouth. The wedding was actually postponed slightly so we had to have a second stag party on the Thursday before it took place, this time back in West Bromwich. Unfortunately Andy couldn't get back from Teignmouth until the following day but we had the party anyway with me standing in for him as 'deputy groom'. The following night was the twenty first birthday of Roy Kramer, another old friend, so by the time Andy's father cooked hamburgers and poured us all gin and tonics on the morning of the wedding, standing was not an activity that could be taken for granted.

During the period of a year or two before the wedding there was a weekly television series called *'Whatever happened to the Likely Lads?'*. The two characters in that series bore striking behavioural resemblances to Andy and I although the events were never confined to one character or the other; there was a lot of both Bob and Terry in both Andy and I although I always remained of the opinion that I was more like Bob and Andy was more like Terry. Decades later, another television series called *'Grumpy Old Men'* appeared and once again Andy and I could clearly see ourselves in the various contributors to those programmes, so what had we become? The irreversible ageing process never stopped us recounting events from our riotous youth every time we met.

The last three occasions, other than his own funeral, at which Andy and I were in the same place at the same time were also funerals; those either of friends or of parents of friends. How particularly sad that was as it was only two holidays, one his and one mine, that prevented us being together on much happier occasions twice more in what was to be his final few weeks of life. Of course there had to be a poem and the one that now follows flowed from my pen on the day of his death. My birthday was three days later but I realised that there would be one card missing from my sideboard that day as, with bitter irony, my cadaverous friend had made my unintended prophecy come true. During my own brush with death several months afterwards, my mind was occupied on the journey to hospital by trying without success to calculate whether or not I had reached a greater age than he did. For the record, I didn't manage that until April 9th 2010.

Some may consider some of these words to be slightly insensitive in the circumstances but, trust me, Andy would have delighted in it so, my dear old mate, this one is just for you – get the beers in, I'll be up (or down) later!

Wharton Minor

My dear cadaverous friend you were
that Christmas, as we had such fun.
Less than eight stones of skin and bones,
mainly bones, but talent by the ton.

The ivories were tickled pink
that evening in the Black Country
and only last week I had a peek
at a book you will never see.

I stood for you in seventy four,
well just about, I do not know how
but that was just the wonder of you
in Teignmouth then as you made your vow.

Likely lads sprang, from time to time,
from grumpy old men we were by then,
often after we had paid respect
to absent friends from way back when.

Now, for the first time since sixty three,
my day will pass without your card
my dear cadaverous friend you are.
You truly are.

I wrote earlier that the poem I had composed to mark the occasion of my son Andrew's wedding to Clare needed very little by way of introduction. Almost precisely one year after that happy event we had another when his little sister Cathy handed me the job of proud father at her wedding to Jonathan.

To bring my 'Father-of-the-Bride' speech to a conclusion, I read another poem which now follows. I have always striven to achieve equivalence in the way I deal with Andrew and Cathy but her poem was for a slightly different purpose, that is to say part of a speech, and therefore in a different style to the classic sonnet form that I used for Andrew's, although both were addressed to them as individuals for the last time before they became part of a married couple. Whilst *'Nuptials'* was self-explanatory, however, I suspect that certain parts of *'Child, Bride'* might need clarifying while other parts have more obvious meanings

When she was a child, Cathy's toes always reminded me of freshly peeled prawns and, to a lesser extent, they still do! During the 1980s, as I prepared to shave each morning before leaving for work, it was Cathy's custom to come into the bathroom to say her first 'Hello Daddy' of the day and I likened this to the story of Aladdin, as her appearance seemed to coincide with the squirt from the aerosol can which contained my shaving foam. I am quite certain that she had more than one night-dress at that time but the one I recall most is a pale yellow one that I think was made by her mother. Until well into her teens she was a thumb-sucker when sleepy. There is a school photograph of her taken in the early part of that phase of life in which she has the angelic look of the little boy on the famous Pear's soap poster that uses Sir John Millais's painting of his grandson. I bought her a flute from my clarinet teacher and, although we learned our respective instruments more or less concurrently, she went down the formal route with examinations as far as Grade Three whereas I did it just for fun and was content to be able to play *'Stranger on the Shore'* and the popular bits of Mozart's *'Clarinet Concerto'* which I first transposed from A Major to C Major to make the fingering easier!

The poem briefly traces her school career at Blackwood and Streetly and then her time studying at Queens Medical Centre as part of her pharmacy degree at Nottingham University. During that time, she met Jonathan Lanes to whom I have now handed over the title of 'Main Man' in her life whilst remaining close at hand to give either or both of them any help, support or advice that they may need.

Child, Bride

My little girl with prawns for toes,
the Genie of the aerosol,
with broken tooth and button nose
and yellow gown and Barbie doll
and big blue eyes and golden hair
and well-sucked thumb and happy face
with gentle dimples here and there,
a Millais portrait framed with lace.

I blinked my eyes and you were dressed
in schoolgirl tunic, bottle green,
competing then with Blackwood's best
and never slacking, always keen.
I blinked again, I often did,
and you had changed some more for me,
no longer just a clever kid,
a teenaged flautist at grade three.

And then the costs began to rise
at QMC (and on the town)
as you worked hard to claim your prize,
a cap and yet another gown.
By then you had a man in mind
to love you in a different way
but look around and you will find
I'll stand behind you every day.

Within a few days of Cathy and Jon's wedding, Denise and I took off to Keswick to enjoy a week of relaxation in the Lake District. We had chosen Keswick by way of a change from Grasmere where we had spent several previous short breaks and we almost immediately came to prefer it.

Walking around the edge of Derwentwater, or boating across it, gives one an irresistible awareness of one's surroundings and I very soon found myself making mental notes of what I was seeing. There are a few small islands in the lake, to which there is no easy or legal access, as if the owners or occupants consider themselves to be separate entities to the surrounding land, isolated from it only by a few feet of water on the surface.

From the windows of the flat we had rented for the week we could see Skiddaw which, at a height of just over three thousand feet, is officially a mountain rather then a hill. Or maybe that is a 'factoid' made up to give the basis of a plot for a Hugh Grant film. There is certainly one school of thought that sets the dividing line at six hundred metres which is of course just under two thousand feet. It did intrigue me to note the smoothness of the surface of Skiddaw's slopes and although that is a quality shared with Cat Bells and other hills, there is a marked contrast between these and the rough surface texture of others such as Walla Crag. I understand that the smooth ones are of sedimentary origin whereas the rough ones owe their existence to volcanic action. There is certainly no difference in the difficulty of climbing them although it must be said that on this particular trip I was carrying about twenty pounds more weight than I do now and I was only a few months away from having a heart attack.

After 'beautiful' I am sure that the next most popular one-word description of the region would be 'peaceful' and so it is most of the time.

However, there are frequent destructions of the peace by Royal Air Force fighter planes apparently on manoeuvres or just practising low flying. As is the case elsewhere, I assume they choose regions such as this because of the relatively low density of population so that fewer people per flight are disturbed by their activities.

Commercial flights to exotic holiday destinations also pass overhead regularly, well out of earshot but on clear days the trails from their engines scar the blue skies; sometimes quite hideously but occasionally quite artistically.

There is also a well-stocked population of real birds and they all make their presence felt from time to time with their calls. It is fascinating to watch geese, about to migrate at that time of year, for all I know, flocking before performing aerobatic synchronised flights low across the lake then soaring high above it while making enough noise to drown out the 'caw caw' noise of those ugly black varieties.

From on high, the tiny boats on the lake look like so many ducks and their sails look like petals, gently borne by a breeze.

Even in late Autumn there is still heat in the Sun which, when doubled by reflections off the lake during a boat trip, can cause some reddening of an unprotected head like mine. Such unseasonable weather can also have an artistic side and the sunsets are quite magnificent, like flames licking the clouds from the tops of the Skiddaw range.

The region has been rich in minerals in the past and the Pencil Museum has become a secondary industry in celebration of the graphite that can be found locally and which was an important export for some time. The cooking ranges of Victorian times, many of them still being in existence, were cleaned or at least smartened up by the surface application of what most including my grandmother called black lead but which was actually graphite. As the name of the museum strongly suggests, however, the principal use of graphite is in pencil making for which the area is renowned.

Then of course there is the lake itself and the streams and rivulets that drain into it and out of it. Some years ago I climbed Ben Nevis, a mountain by any definition, equipped only with one half-litre bottle of water. Not being much of a water drinker I thought that would be enough to sustain me during an eight hour day in the middle of summer while climbing 4406 feet into the sky, and back. It was, after all, half a litre more water than I drink most days. Twenty minutes into the climb I had to refill the bottle from a stream and I repeated the process three times per hour for the rest of the day. Around Derwentwater I noticed that both the joggers and the anorak types were always clutching branded water bottles but I never saw anyone filling one from the natural supply.

The surface of the lake can from time to time become almost mirror-like but never for very long as even the smallest duck causes ripples that can reach from side to side.

212

When one of the ferries that ply from point to point around the lake goes by, the waves created are surprisingly intense and smaller vessels are tossed wildly by their wakes and bow-waves.

One evening during dinner at a fish restaurant overlooking Keswick's market place, it occurred to me that the thoughts I have summarised above could be divided readily into four distinct categories, loosely connected to each other by some gentle abstract force.

This realisation in turn put me in mind of the beliefs of several ancient civilisations, notably the Greeks, who held that everything in the World whether animal, vegetable or mineral, was made up of the combination in differing proportions of only four elements: Earth, Air, Fire and Water.

Having been re-introduced recently into the joys of the Periodic Table of the Elements as a result of Denise setting out to fill a small gap in her education, I think those old boys had a good point. Apart from the difficulty I would have in stringing together a dozen lines that make things like beryllium sound interesting and romantic, there would have to be over a hundred verses in such a poem to fit all of the now-known elements in!

How strange, I thought, that my own categories of thoughts and observations could easily be annotated in the same way and that the abstract force that linked each to the others could as easily be the Aether that those people of old thought of as perhaps not quite a fifth element but at the very least a fundamental compound that acts as a catalyst for the interaction of the 'big four'.

I don't have a name for my force but if I did, perhaps it would be something like 'human sensual perceptiveness' which in this day and age would become universally known by the acronym HSP.

What I do have as a product of that holiday are four free verse poems which I have grouped together to form what I call *'Elements of Keswick'*.

Earth, Air, Fire and Water:
Elements of Keswick

Small islands stand aloof,
pretending independence
but connected, out of sight,
to earth that rises from the flat to hills,
perhaps a mountain or two.
Some rough, like Walla Crag,
some Olay smooth, like Skiddaw.
Enchanted, we rise too, following paths
which are also crossed
by slithered tree roots
like sleeping snakes,
perhaps the fossils of tomorrow.

Above it all, the atmosphere
is clean and crisp and clear
despite the angry Harriers, flying low,
and the vapour trails of soaring silver birds.
Rowdy rooks or ravens
are oft-times shouted down by barking geese
flying in formation, just for fun,
below the creamy clouds of clotted air.
Lazy breezes blow, now and again,
and empower the panting sails,
which look like lily petals loosely fixed
to masts on mallards, bobbing over there.

The incandescent ball sends down its rays,
despite the time of year,
causing minor burning of tender skin
on unprotected heads; no hat nor hair.
It fires the inspiration, brings the muse,
with flames on the horizon
as the day retires
to let the evening have its way.
Eruptions from the inferno are long dead
but coal is there for us to burn again
and graphite too, for making ovens black
and giving poets such a useful tool.

Six thousand million gallons, give or take,
lie there, stirring but unstirred,
and slake the thirst of all who come to drink,
constantly filled and drained by cool, clear streams.
Yet walkers, anorak-clad and all with dogs in tow,
and runners, all in spandex, some go fast, some slow
forsake the chance to sup from nature's cup,
taking water from bottles bearing foreign names.
Gentle little dinghies, not really ducks,
skim across the rippled surface of the lake,
from time to time becalmed
then tossed by bow waves from the bigger boats.

First published in The Dawntreader. Summer 2010. Issue 011

During the course of any given month I read a lot of poems. Half of them have been written for many years and I have read at least half of those many times before but I still enjoy them.

However, I also read a great deal of new poems written both by professionals and by amateurs who, like me, have the occasional scribbling published in various poetry magazines and anthologies. Several of the poems in this book have been published previously in this way. However, I find that I have to search long and hard for new poems that I can both admire and enjoy. There are some poems that I can admire and there are many poems that I can enjoy, but there is only a small few that can tick both boxes for me.

At this stage in the book, I sincerely hope that any reader still hanging on for the end will have had both boxes ticked by my work at least once or twice! What I mean to say is that I find it very hard indeed to admire a poem that has no recognisable form and is in reality little more than a list of randomly connected words. Worse still there are the poems that I referred to earlier as 'chopped up prose'. A line end should at the very least be a type of punctuation as would a comma, colon or full stop. Alternatively, it may be the place for a rhyme or it may be the place at which the natural rhythm of the poem needs to break. It may also be the place at which a rigid form of poetry such as a sonnet needs a line end; in the example of the sonnet there must be ten syllable sounds to each of fourteen lines and there are strict rhyming patterns, one of which should be followed although I often don't. But by now I am sure you are painfully aware of that even if you weren't at the start.

I do not object to free verse as such, as is evident from the previous poem, but it is hard to write it well and in many cases it would be better presented as prose. The quality is not improved by silly devices such as missing out all capital letters or definite articles and some writers even start new stanzas for no apparent reason.

Anyway, my point is that I like my poems to have some sense of direction and the ways that this can be achieved are so numerous that there is no excuse not to use one or other of them, in my view.

I once read a brief article on the rubai. Like most people, I suspect, I was more accustomed to seeing the word in its plural form, rubaiyat. Moreover, I would have been quite unable to name any rubaiyat other than those attributed to Omar Khayyam but which were translated from the original

216

Persian by Edward Fitzgerald and which I suspect were as much the work of the translator as they were the original author. I did much the same thing myself some years ago with the works of Empress Elisabeth of Austria-Hungary who, had she lived another hundred years or so to read them, would never have recognised her poems after I had re-translated, modernised and titled them. I refer of course to *'The Sisi Set'* which, for this book, I have extended from its originally published version by adding a few newly re-written poems from the great lady.

Rubai is in essence the old Persian word for the number four and, apart from being responsible, in one of my own theories of life, for the use of the word 'rubber' in the four- player card game of bridge, means a four line poem or a four line verse or stanza in a longer poem called a rubaiyat.

As with most poetic forms, there are other rules but also variations. One of these has come to be called the interlocking rubaiyat which can have any number of rubai provided that each has four lines of ten syllable sounds and that the first, second and fourth lines have end rhymes. To interlock, the sound of the third line end of the first rubai rhymes with the first, second and fourth end lines of the second rubai and so on until the last rubai, in which the third line end rhymes with the first, second and fourth line ends of the first rubai.

My one and only use of this form follows, the subject matter being aligned with the work of some of the Romantic poets of the eighteenth and nineteenth centuries. For that reason alone I have called it *'Rubaiyat for Romantics'* I wonder how many of your boxes it will tick!

Rubaiyat for Romantics

Rage can be a corollary of grief,
accusing curses thrown to bring relief.
Our pain is often eased by moving blame
and snatching absolution, like a thief.

If we can treat impostors all the same,
the thought with which Old Rudyard made his name,
and keep our feet still rooted in the earth,
then deeds of others need not bring us shame.

For those who love the planet of their birth
and wonder why the rest dispute its worth,
the sky, the sea, the mountains and the lakes
are splendid sights of which there is no dearth.

In Winter-time the beauty is in flakes,
each one a very different pattern makes
but lying altogether form a quilt
or blanket holding warmth till Spring awakes.

And Summer presses pleasure to the hilt
but Autumn's beauty comes when woodlands wilt.
With days of sunshine growing ever brief
as longer nights approach us at full tilt.

Monday 1st February 2010 was the start of National Heart Awareness month in the UK but I didn't know that until a few days later. As with every workday morning at the time, the heating system at home came to life at 7.00 a.m. and as usual woke me with the noise of water tanks, pipes and radiators warming up and piercing the almost perfect silence that otherwise we enjoy most of the time. At 7.25 a.m. the alarm of my cell phone activates and plays the sound of what I think are blackbirds; certainly the sound is similar to that which, if our bedroom window is left open, I hear from the blackbirds which nest in our laurel hedge. The next step in this daily ritual is for me to activate the television using the remote control on my bedside table, so that I can hear any overnight news and sports results before getting up to make breakfast.

On this particular day I suddenly felt very ill and decided to go downstairs immediately. As the kettle boiled I felt worse and, as soon as I could manage it, I went back upstairs to get help or comfort from Denise. We both realised quickly that I was in the throes of a heart attack and so the emergency services were called. With impressive speed I was given such treatment that was possible before being transported, with blue lights flashing and sirens wailing, to hospital where a surgeon was waiting to clear the blockage in one of my arteries and to insert a stent to reduce the risk of it blocking again.

Before noon, the operation was over and I was admitted to a ward with three other chaps in similar circumstances. I have often been a severe critic of the National Health Service but my experience in this matter has modified my views to some extent and I am convinced that, without the excellent treatment I was given that day and subsequently, I would have surely died.

After a welcome lunch of hospital food, I can't be more specific as to what it was, I felt quite good despite being wired up and plumbed from every existing orifice and several newly created ones. However, the mystery dish filled me with trapped wind and this put me in mind of the carnage of the Somme on 1st July 1916 so that afternoon I wrote *'The Attack'* .

The Attack

It was oh-seven-thirty hours on the first of the month.
Five minutes earlier there had been birdsong as usual
after the distant rumble of tanks before dawn.
I heard no whistles but the attack commenced
and I knew then why my wire had been cut.

Then the medics came and took me to a safer place
away for now from friend and foe.
From old friends only, as I soon found new.
Food of a type I once thought meagre was very welcome now
and filled my plate with homely warmth
but my stomach with gas, like a dead man rotting.

But I am not a German soldier.
I was nowhere near the Somme.
It is no longer July 1916.

This attack was personal!

First published in Reach Poetry. Issue 139. April 2010

The final poem doesn't really need any introduction nor any explanation. It is nothing more than simple, cynical comment on the packaging of just about every food product these days, which includes advice as to what arbitrary date the contents suddenly become toxic.

In earlier, more sensible, times we used to visually inspect the bottle of milk or the loose wrapped boiled ham and, if in any doubt as to its edibility after that, we used to sniff it. The absence of any bad odour was usually enough to declare the product fresh enough to eat or drink.

I was never a big drinker of water, or corporation pop as it was sometimes called by my less than affluent friends, but when an hour or two of football or other such energetic pastime in the park forced me to use the drinking fountain (supplied by the corporation) it never occurred to me to look at it or smell it before taking a few slurps and getting on with the game in hand.

It struck me as being on the ludicrous side of amusing a few years ago to read a label on a bottle of water that extolled the purity of the contents by claiming that it had taken tens of thousands of years to filter through the finest rock in Scotland before being bottled but that if you dared to take one sip after a certain date a few weeks hence then you would instantly fall to the ground retching and writhing in agony before dying a slow and painful death. Actually it wasn't quite as dramatic as that but you know what I mean.

For the poem, **'Best before'**, the arbitrary date that I chose just happened to be my mother's birthday. I added a couple of verses to make the point on behalf of fruit and meat whilst leading to the main point which is that this lump of semi-molten rock that we inhabit, and all that is found naturally upon it, will do as it will without a care for what humans do while we are here. As I have said before in relation to my poem **'Climate Change'**, the native Americans had it summed up with their proverb which I will quote again now.

'The mountains laugh when they see men fighting over who owns them'.

Best before

Nature doesn't have a best-by date
to put upon its many product lines
and water filtered for a million years
through rock and sand and then drunk, unrefined,
will not be 'best before the tenth of May'.

Apples plucked with care from straining boughs
and stored alone in darkness, undisturbed,
can still be eaten with the festive fayre
or when the snow has gone and blossom grows,
a sign of next year's bounty from the land.

Both fish and flesh will also last until
they are replaced by nature's turning wheel
if they are seasoned well with Gaia's salt
or smoked above the smould'ring embers of
the tired trees that now provide our warmth.

This precious earth, and many others too,
are timeless, ageless and beyond the power
of mortal species, newly born, to end
by foul abuse of buried oil and gas.
Nature doesn't have a best-by date.

First published in Reach Poetry October 2010. Issue number 145